MORNING COFFEE WITH GOD

by Michael Dennis

For permission, serialization, condensation, adaptions, or for our catalog of other publications, write to Ozark Mountain Publishing, Inc., P.O. box 754, Huntsville, AR 72740, ATTN: Permissions Department.

Library of Congress Cataloging-in-Publication Data

Dennis, Michael, 1957-
  Morning Coffee with God, by Michael Dennis
A regular dialog with God discussing living life on Earth.

1. Metaphysics   2. God   3. Life Issues   4. Channeling
I. Dennis, Michael, 1957-   II. Metaphysics   III. Title

Library of Congress Catalog Card Number: 2010921666

ISBN: 978-1-886940-68-0

Cover Art and Layout: www.enki3d.com
Book set in: Times New Roman, Invitation
Book Design: Julia Degan

Published by:

PO Box 754
Huntsville, AR 72740

WWW.OZARKMT.COM
Printed in the United States of America

Acknowledgements:

I wish to thank Miss Leiah Kitare, my good Cincinnati , OH friend and fellow psychic of twenty-five years, for all of her help in improving Morning Coffee With God. She spent many hours over lunch listening to chapters and helping to hone the book. She caught typos, grammar, and little things that I missed and her scanning ability and feel for flow is impeccable. She psychically picked up that this book would be published. Thanks for believing and encouraging me and for being a good friend. A most sincere thanks. Love and hugs, Michael

I also wish to extend a big hearty thanks to Arielle, in Indianapolis , Indiana . She stuck with me all of the way and read the chapters more than once, offering many helpful suggestions on ways to improve the book. She has such a way with words and her editing skills are impeccable. Arielle, I look forward to reading your channeled book by Mary Magdalene when you get it done. Love and hugs, Michael

To Sweet Viktoria Kree,
Although your spirit and soul have soared to the heavens of your starry origins, you are always in my heart. Thanks for being there for me during the writing and the 'rewriting' of Morning Coffee With God. Your loving, encouraging emails were what kept me going when I got discouraged. Your suggestions and many pointers and observations helped improve the book. You are a wonderful and dear, mentor, friend, and soul mate to me. You taught me how to hone my writing and psychic skills, and equally important 'the business aspect' of learning to make a living as a Psychic. Thanks to you, I am unstoppable now!" I am sending you the first copy via the Heaven Express. I can never thank you enough. Love, Michael

Contents

Prologue

Morning Coffee With God was written during the winter of 2005. I was taking a sabbatical for a few months and stayed with my friend Leiah Kitare in Cincinnati, OH. She lives near the Ohio river in an old house built in the 1890's and was in the process of renovating her house.

The book was spurred by a series of dreams that took place in the wee hours of the morning, but a few occurred when I took naps in the afternoon or early evening. I was astonished with the consistency of the dreams and my ability to recall the conversations near verbatim when I awoke, along with the depth and penetrating insights of the conversations and writings.

Introduction

I reread my book and still I was not satisfied. I kept thinking, this story is a bit or perhaps way out there. Yet it is what I experienced, so how can I deny it? Nonetheless, I still could not shake off the feeling that I might be labeled "a madman" should I dare attempt to share it. I even considered not sending the book to publishers even though Mr. Divine had mentioned more than once that I was not writing the book merely for myself; he also predicted that others would benefit from it. Needless to say, I struggled.

The domain of dreams is not unfamiliar territory to me. I have been a spiritual counselor for over twenty years and dream analysis/interpretation is one of the areas I work in. But to claim to have "morning coffee visits" with God? Isn't that kind of audacious even if I claim to have them in dreams? How could I possibly expect anyone to believe such a story? How could I expect myself to believe it? The struggle continued. I wanted to share my dreams, but I could not get motivated or bring myself to do it. I would read the copious notes I took and be filled with all the original excitement and yet I kept that excitement to myself. I even had fantasies of deleting the file from my computer.

As fate would have it, a dream is what kept me from pushing the delete key. One night I dreamt I was in a classroom sitting alone at a desk. I wondered if I was serving detention. A petite perky lady enters the classroom. "Why am I here?" I asked her. She looked at me, then said "Michael, you did not do your homework."

"My homework?" I asked incredulously. "I always do my homework."

She shook her head and pointed at me. "Okay then, so what is my homework?" I asked.

She went to the chalkboard and wrote four words in big capital letters – SEND YOUR BOOK OUT then added, "And you know which one." She disappeared and the dream ended. *Well, so much for not sending the book out to publishers*, I thought. *I wonder if they will all think I'm nuts?* I decided to consult a friend who had read parts of the book and ask his opinion. Here is what he said:

"Michael, I feel the story is very rich with spiritual substance: however, I think it would be good to develop the theme of "incredulity" a little more. Because you are at this time a little more familiar with encounters of the spirit than most, you quickly adjust to the stunning circumstances of having God come for morning coffee with you. I believe that most people would go through various stages of disbelief and mistrust of their own senses. I realize that this encounter was characterized as a "dream journey"– and then some – but I opine that some readers will still struggle with the story because they just can't get past the phenomenon of direct contact with God-dream or not. I respectfully suggest that you give these folks permission to ride along a bit, too. You might say something like:

"Dear Reader, I do not expect you to swallow this! In fact, it was *my* experience, and yet as I look back upon it, I still have moments of doubt – doubt that it really happened, doubt of my own sanity – and I often wonder about the 'reality' that surrounds me during my waking hours today!

"But please indulge me here. It is of little concern to me whether you think I am 'off my rocker'. I will leave it up to you to decide whether the circumstances I describe are rooted in rock-solid, day-to-day living, or if they are musings of a man who spends too much time talking with himself. I would be disappointed if your incredulity caused you to overlook the message in *His* words. Just this once, allow yourself to play a game of 'let's pretend' long enough to hear what Mr. Divine is saying!"

The struggle continued for months. It felt like I had become two different people. The battles between my mind and heart were ongoing, and many times it was so tempting to take the notes and burn them to ashes.

However, I also know that sometimes we must throw caution to the wind – that is if we want to grow and expand our horizons. I thought of the scene in Shirley Maclaine's book, *Out On A Limb,* where it says to get to the fruit you have to go out on a limb. One of my favorite poems is called, "Risking". It ends by saying we are only free if we take risks.

After a long struggle, I finally decided to go forward with the book. I went out on a limb. I took a risk. I trusted and followed my intuition even though I was scared out of my wits because my comfort zone was constantly being invaded and my beliefs challenged. So it is with no regrets and with much pleasure that I say "In a magical place somewhere in time, I shared my first cup of coffee with God."

Chapter One

The Initial Visit

I was not sure if I had fallen asleep or if I was in that half-dream-half-awake state. It was still early in the morning, not yet daybreak. I rolled over into a comfortable position and snuggled into the blankets. My face still felt chilled, so I buried myself deeper into the warmth of the covers. Suddenly I felt the weight of something sit down on the bed. I could smell the different scent, and I could hear soft even breathing. I tried to open my eyes and to move; I could do neither. Panicking, I kept trying to move just anything; something was not right. What was happening? I was praying that this was just a dream that I would soon awaken from.

My eyes seemed to belong to someone else. My hands were sweating and clammy. Feeling half-numb, I became aware of something or someone beside me. My breath caught in my chest and each additional one became a struggle. What was happening? "Help me, please help me," I kept silently pleading. An eternity seemed to pass by. Was I having a stroke? Was my heart failing? Was I dying? Questions crossed the blackboard of my mind. I felt something like a hand lay on my shoulder; still unable to open my eyes or move, but somehow feeling it. A gentle kind of relaxing sensation softly filled my body; my eyes began to open. The brilliant light was all that I could see; it was as if I were lying in the midst of a stalled lightning flash. How can I explain this when it was like nothing I have ever seen or experienced? Slowly, the brilliant light dimmed and I glimpsed a tenuous shadowy form sitting on my bed.

The light was becoming more natural and my eyes were adjusting. I was trying to make out the hazy figure on the bed beside me while rubbing my eyes and looking again. Suddenly, I could see the figure and my heart almost stopped beating. Fear and terror took over; this could not be real. My mouth tried to form words but it was impossible, until *HE* touched my face soothingly and said, "Do not fear."

Our eyes locked. I sensed that the stranger was not here to do me harm. A few moments later, he spoke softly, "Michael, I am God."

My mouth dropped; my head began spinning, and I thought I might faint. I even wondered if I had been drugged. I closed my eyes, hoping he would simply disappear. Perhaps I was only dreaming. A smile formed on his face and he reached out his hand to me. I winced and backed away.

"Who did you say you were?" I finally managed to stutter.

He looked at me with his intense penetrating blue eyes. Tingles poured through my entire being. His intense gaze held my eyes. I could feel dizziness overtaking me and my body going numb. He smiled, then said in a soft voice, "Michael, I am God."

I stared at him, speechless. It's one thing to talk about something so different; so far out that it challenges our beliefs and everything we were taught in church. Conversation or reading a book can be stimulating and educational, but it is not the same thing as direct experience. A pleasant memory came to mind. I had made almond chocolate fudge one day and had told a friend about it. "What does it taste like?" she asked. "I don't know," I had replied. "I can't tell you what it tastes like. You have to experience it for yourself." Experience it for yourself. The thought petrified me. What comfort was that? That's like somebody telling you that once you take the big plunge into the pool from the high dive that it's all down hill from there. Or someone telling you that once you jump out of the plane, your parachute will activate and you will land safely.

What consolation are words when you are standing alone on the high dive, or staring out the airplane shivering, heart pounding like a drum, fearing you are about to plunge to your death? What if your parachute does not activate? At that moment, I was so barraged by trembling and terror I thought I might pass out. This was just too much. How did I know this was not some ruse or trap? "Be ever on the alert, even the devil mixes the truth with lies so as to ensnare and confuse you." I recalled Pastor Cleveland often saying in sermons when I was a kid. Could this character be a demon in disguise? I looked at him again. He certainly did not look like one. Lord knows that one of my favorite sayings is "looks can be deceiving". I stole another glance in his direction. His eyes were so penetratingly deep and ethereal blue. He looked young and old at the same time. I did not sense that he was evil. Hadn't I listened to my intuition before when sizing people up? The bottom line was that I was almost always right. My first impressions are usually accurate and my first impression was that whoever he was, there was not an ounce of meanness in him. I took some comfort in that thought, then managed to get out with difficulty, "Please tell me that this is all a joke, or better still, just a dream."

He smiled and spoke gently. "Michael, this is no joke, but it *is* a type of dream. But do not be fooled. Dreams have their own reality and there are many different types of dreams."

My teeth were clattering and my knees shaking. It felt like electrical currents were going through every limb and fiber of my being. As though sensing my state of mind which was half-shock and half-terror, he repeated himself. "Michael, this is no joke; it *is* a type of dream. But don't be fooled. Dreams have their own reality. You have been engaged in a very active dream life for many years. For now, why don't we sit by the fireplace? It is lovely you know. Nothing would please me more than to have morning coffee with you."

I tried to reply, but the overwhelming magnitude of this presence made me fear that I was losing my grip on reality. Was this real? I kept asking myself. *He* says it is a dream, but it seems so real. I finally quit trying to stop the shaking and trembling and just let my body move as it willed. I felt like a rag doll with no control whatsoever.

This very unusual stranger gave me a look of kindness that I had never before seen. There seemed to be a golden radiant glow around him; I could even feel the warmth. His kind smile calmed me a little. I found myself thinking, *am I about to have a cup of coffee with the Divine Almighty? What is it like to share a cup of coffee with a being so magnificent? No, this couldn't be. I cannot be having this dream.*

He spoke softly. "Don't resist, Michael. Trust your feelings about me. Time is of the utmost essence and there is much to share and teach you. Now let me say it once more, nothing would please me more than to have morning coffee with you; that would be a taste of 'heaven on earth' as I know you are quite the connoisseur of fine coffees."

He touched me gently on the cheek and gave me another of his magical smiles. For a moment it felt like every hurt that I carried inside had been instantly healed. The woes of the world did not seem real; as a matter of fact, the outside world seemed like a dream. I wanted to look into his eyes and lose myself and forget every trouble I had ever had. I had never felt so safe as I felt being with him.

After I finally adjusted to *His* presence, I pointed a trembling finger towards my kitchen and asked, "Do you really wish for a cup of coffee?" He replied with a nod of his head. As I walked down the hallway, I thought to myself how happy I was that I had thick soft carpet for him to walk on. The freshly painted sky blue walls seemed to show off their beauty; the morning sunlight was filtering through the kitchen. I know that it was my imagination and the magic of the moment, but the refrigerator and stove seemed to gleam; it was almost as if we were standing among the clouds. Quickly, I pulled out the chair at the head of the table and motioned for *HIM* to sit.

Now, it just hit me – I was going to make a cup of coffee for God. How do I do this? How can I just make a cup of coffee for someone so immense, so visibly supreme I wondered as my breath came in short huffs, and my hands twitched nervously?

Taking a couple of deep breaths, I slowly calmed myself down. I went to the freezer and grabbed the Kona Coffee Beans. My friend Leiah said she liked Hawaiian kona beans better than the Jamaican blue mountain. If you know good coffee, then you automatically connect Kona with good coffee, so kona it would be.

The coffee grinder was noisy and I wished I could just hurry it up. I did not want the noise, but the results would be well worth it. Filling the pot with filtered bottled water was the first thing that I did. Next, I measured ground Kona Coffee and put it in the filter, pulled the lid down and pressed the start button.

The kitchen seemed to become a jet. I felt as if I were high in the clouds. The world seemed to be distantly far from me; it was just me and this awesome supreme guest. I settled into the chair across from *HIM* and watched as *HE* looked around the room with contentment.

Soon the rich robust aroma of coffee filled the room. *HE* sniffed and sighed, a sign that he was enjoying this scent; I realized that neither of us had spoken. Perhaps it was just not time. I'm seldom at a loss for words, but now I was shivering inside with excitement, and anxiousness. Was I scared? No, that is not the word – terrified is a better word for what was going on inside me. I was sure that *HE* could hear my heart beating. It sounded like an amazon drum....hurry coffee, hurry coffee was all I could think.

Finally, the last gurgle of the dripping coffee sounded and I leaped towards the cups and began pouring. Cream and sugar were already on the table. I sat down again holding both hands around the steaming cup of coffee as if they were cold and needed warming.

I waited what seemed to be an eternity. *HE* took several sips and seemed to bask in the rich taste of the hot steamy liquid. *HE* then put the cup down, clasped both hands together on the table and looked deeply into my eyes, and began speaking.

"What are you thinking?" he asked softly.

"Do you really want to know?" I asked with hesitation and a little embarrassment.

"Of course I do."

"To be perfectly honest, I'm depressed."

"So do you want undepressed?"

Undepressed, I thought. *I don't think I've heard that word before.*

HE simply looked at me and repeated himself. "Do you want

undepressed or to put it in your vernacular to not be depressed?"

So many rambling thoughts poured into my head. There was so much I wanted to ask him, but I decided to avoid his question and ask him one instead. Why not start with the most commonly asked question on the planet?

"How are you?"

He grinned, then spoke softly. "I am wonderful. Absolutely wonderful."

"That is great, but can you tell me why am I so depressed?"

"Yes I can. You are depressed because you avoid me. You put a-void between you and me. Do you want out of the pit or do you want to keep feeling pitiful?"

I did not comment. I was quiet a few moments, then ventured to ask "Why are you here?"

"Because you have been reaching out and calling to me in dreams. Divine contact from dreams may be uncommon, but it is not unheard of."

"I called out to you?" I asked, surprised.

He grinned. Yes you did, just like you called out to the angel who paid you a visit many years ago and inspired you to write *The Messenger of Love*.

"You mean that dream was real and she really was an angel?"

"Yes, just as this dream is real. Actually, Michael, I have been with you before. Many times. And not just in this dream."

"Can't you stop reminding me that I am dreaming?" I wanted to say. Let me enjoy what seems so very real. Even the scent of the coffee. It all seems real."

I looked at him. He was smiling. "Let me help you recall some times you have talked to me. How about when you were eleven years old, waiting for Geneva Jackson to pick you up for church? You talked to me a lot back then. You asked me to take you away from your dysfunctional home and violent father, and you told me you wanted to go to college. You told me how much you loved me and you even went so far as to say you wanted to meet me someday."

My eyes lit up. "I do remember that. I used to pray a lot and I was a big dreamer way back then when I was only eleven years old. When things were so bad at home, I'd retreat to the back yard and close my eyes and say, 'It's all just a dream. A nightmare in the daytime.' Then I'd open my eyes and hope that it would all be gone. Sometimes I even convinced myself that it was. I guess I had a very vivid imagination."

"Your imagination has served you well and continues to do so."

"Thank you. So are you real?"

"Look at me and observe and then decide for yourself."

There I was sitting at the table with the most Supreme Being, the ultimate guest. Questions swirled in my mind as I took in this most incredible sight. God sipped his coffee, his ringless fingers wrapped warmly around *HIS* cup. *He* was dressed in white trousers and a white linen shirt with small blue buttons with long sleeves covering *HIS* arms. I could feel concern dwelling deep within *HIS* steady gaze. I had never seen such beautiful eyes. They were a mysterious sort of sky blue with a silver tint. They looked like they had seen worlds upon worlds time and time again, and things I could probably never fathom. I wondered what journeys I would take and what I would see if I lost myself in *HIS* eyes. But today *HE* was here looking at me, and my heart was missing at least every other beat.

I stammered, "Do you have a lesson that you want to share with me, teach me, or talk to me about? May I ask questions? Will I ever see you again? Will I see where you live? Is there an eternity?" My mouth was moving non-stop, as if *He* may just disappear and I would not have a chance to ask *Him*.

God smiled at me. *His* eyes reverted to the window, and as *He* looked out, *He* began, "Destruction, tidal waves, bombings, wars, hurricanes, crashes. Do you really think these are my doings – that I purposely create these destructive devastations? Is this what you hear, and read and believe?"

The question startled me so much that I sat there unable to respond, unable to speak, actually unable to think clearly. How do I respond to a question of such magnitude? The shock on my face was reply enough, I soon learned.

He continued, "The Earth was created ? cold, warmth, land, water, vegetation, minerals. The earth evolves around the beauty of the giant sequoia trees, the majestic oceans, the vast lands. The earth has forces of nature that man cannot control. Now war, famine, hunger – these are not forces of nature and man can control them. Why do so many of your rich people who have millions of dollars not share their wealth with the poor and the hungry? You have the capabilities to make lives equal, but instead, you generate your lives toward greed and personal wealth. Why are people so reluctant to share? These are matters that we must talk about, understand, and one day, you will reveal our conversations to those who will offer an ear.

"The being sitting here beside you is more than a figment of your imagination. We could go on for hours discussing 'more than,' but we will not go there today. For now, let me just say that I can take on any form I wish on any plane or dimension, of which the earth plane is only one among many. And likewise, the realm of dreams has many dimensions. "

HE picked up *His* coffee cup and held it firmly in *His* hands, then took a big sip and let out a sigh. "Your kona brew is the best." *He* looked towards the kitchen, then moved *His* chair and bent slightly in my direction. My head began to feel giddy. "Earlier we were talking about other times I talked to you. Do you want to hear of any more?"

"Oh yes, please."

"In May of 1984, in the wee hour of the morn, you scribbled a page of disjointed thoughts which you later rewrote and named it *Message from my Soul.* The wee morning hours are a good time to communicate with me because the mind does not get in the way nearly as much. That was one of our early communications."

"I recall that day very well. I was love-struck and although Cupid had pierced my heart pretty deeply, the love was not reciprocated. Unrequited love is dreadful. What lonely years those were! I guess I've always been part-loner and probably always will be. At an early age, the so-called "normal life" was not enough for me. The characters and adventures of my inner world have always been as important to me as the ones in the so-called real world. Perhaps something deep in my soul just resonates to such communications. I felt at that moment what Joan of Arc must have felt when her voices spoke to her. How they must have given her such hope and comfort. How it felt so natural and normal that they should visit and speak with her. How she must have loved them. Am I making sense, God?"

"I would like for you to call me Mr. Divine. It sure beats you saying *HE* or *God* and besides *God* is not, nor has it ever been my true or total name. Actually, somebody just made up that name. So why not make up another one a little less formal and perhaps more pleasant sounding? The name God elicits strong feelings and reactions from people – both pleasant and unpleasant. Due to the lack of understanding of who I am, and the abuses and atrocities that have been committed in my name, some disbelieve that I even exist. As a matter of fact, I don't even believe in *God* if you want my honest opinion."

"So who did I speak and pray to all those lonely childhood years?"

"I am That I am. That is closer to my real name, but for now, I would like for you to call me Mr. Divine."

"Why does everybody call you *God* and say you are the almighty Supreme Being and creator of the universe?"

"For a lot of reasons we do not have time to go into now. Let's just say that the titles I have been assigned reflect such a minute part and fraction of who I am. I am so much more and so are you. For the purpose of these visits, to you I will be Mr. Divine."

"I'm okay with that."

"I'm Okay, You're okay," he said, smiling. "That was a good book that helped you a lot."

"It sure did. My Psychology books have served me well over the years."

"Psychology is fascinating and before we're through, you might even be able to out shrink the shrinks," Mr. Divine said, smiling. "If Psychology helps bring you back to yourself, then I endorse it. It is my hope and desire that you discover that sacred place in your heart where love dwells. There are endless means to get there. Once you come to realize that I love you, you are well on your way to getting there."

"Are you really talking to me now?" I couldn't resist asking.

"No, I'm talking to the man standing behind you. Seriously, I've been talking to you for some time, but you forget when you wake up. I will let you in on a little secret. I have been contacting you for many years at the deeper levels of sleep. That is why for years you sometimes wake up with deep questions on your mind. It is those dream visits that put you in your 'deep moods'. Since most people cannot recall what occurs at the deep levels of sleep, you had no conscious recollection of them having taken place.

"Let's say that your recollections have been subconscious recollections, and as you know from your studies in Psychology, the contents and the workings of your subconscious mind do influence you; and you, more so than the average person because of your heightened sensitivity. Now it is time to get to the root of those yearnings so you don't have to be bombarded with feelings of loneliness as you seek and search for something that you can't define or put your hands on. It is time for knowledge to liberate you and for you to find peace. Haven't you been seeking peace of mind and heart for years?"

"Yes, all of my life."

"Like your book, *Halfway to Heaven,* says, "The call compels the response." If you believe in peace and seek it, then it must exist, for how can you seek something that is non-existent? If it were non-existent, or readily outside your field of perception, then you could not seek it for it would not be real to you. Just as your shaman therapist used to remind you of the power of your despair and dark depressions and the need to confront and learn from them; likewise do your hidden yearnings possess much power and many gifts for you. Yearning is so intense and powerful because it is your soul's attempt to get your attention. When you are out of sync, this means that you are not following your bliss. When you are not following your bliss, you are not in the flow. You are not being true to your self; this stirs the yearnings that fill you with sadness and longing. Think of the yearnings as a little alarm going off or a wake-up call to alert you that all is not so well on the home front. People go for years being depressed, sad and lonely, thinking they are doomed to despair. Many come to expect it just as one gets used to the cold weather and ice in the wintertime.

"Nothing could be further from the truth. How sad when people give up hope that life *can be* joyous and fulfilling. Some even go so far as to deny their unhappiness. They will say things like 'Life is rough, you just accept what is. You do the best you can and accept what you can't change.' Unfortunately, people come to accept the things they believe they cannot change, when in reality most of them they can change. To live a life of desperation is to be untrue to the self.

"Your true soul calling is to learn to fully love 'self and others' and to spread that love profusely. Another of your soul callings is to fully awaken your creativity and fully embrace your muse. She, who is the spirit of your inspiration, will help you surrender to your soul, for as your internal twin flame and divine counterpart, she cannot be fulfilled until you are. She needs you as much as you need her. So, of course, you have been depressed and lonely most of your life; your yearnings have been your constant reminders that something is awry and in need of fixing. The good news is that once you come to embrace your internal muse (your divine feminine counterpart), you will meet someone on the physical external realm who will be a mirror for your internal muse. It is the love of the divine internal counterpart that everyone seeks and who they must discover within, then bond and merge with before they meet someone externally who can mirror their true being. We will get into this subject more when we explore your 'writing' *On Love.*

"I am happy to say that you are embracing your muse more. You are willing to do some more inner healing work and to get to the root of your 'yearnings'. You are ready to become more true to yourself. Your soul has always known that contact with divinity is not only possible, but available to everyone. No one can be truly happy until this contact is made.

"You are going to remember our talks and they will become the foundation for a book. Your dream life is going to become quite active. In truth, you are in a dream like frame of mind when you write your poems, songs, fantasy stories and novels. When you do a reading for a client, you are taking a soul journey with them which is similar to dreaming. On your journeys, you have access to much more information and knowledge than is accessible to your conscious mind. You have access to the subconscious and super-conscious mind. With practice, there is no knowledge you cannot access for it is stored in the very DNA of your genetic makeup and in your cells and molecules. And since you and everyone on the planet are soul connected, you can access their subconscious and super-conscious mind as well as the universal mind. You can essentially become omniscient just like me. You have been doing quite well. Surely you realize that your spiritual work is much more than predictions and fortune telling?"

"I've been told that it goes much deeper than that."

"It does and since you have been restless for some time, I thought I'd offer a little help. I decided it was time to make an official appearance that you wouldn't forget and to inspire you to get back to your writing. That is another reason you are depressed. You are not writing! Writing is very healing for you. It puts you in touch with your soul. Your soul can speak more clearly through the written word since it is a skill that you have developed in many previous lives. Writing has always been easy and natural for you. You have made much progress and improvement over the years and are continually doing so.

"It is time for you to get back to your writing. You have so many books inside you yearning to see the light of day. Speaking of your writing, I know about your past lives as a writer and I drew upon that knowledge when I helped rouse you in those wee hours of the morn back in May of 1984 in your throes and woes times. I helped your super-conscious or your higher self make a connection with you. I know it was very unsettling and a bit of a shock to you, but it had to happen. You were getting too lost, and the darkness was overshadowing you. Your soul called out for help in dream time.

"You have called out for help other times and one such time led to your writing *The Messenger of Love* – given to you from an angel who taught you about unconditional love. When you asked her why she appeared, she reminded you that you called out to her in dream time."

"I recall that dream and 'writing' very well. It was so real. It seemed like much more than a dream and I confess that at first I did not like it. I was too caught up with my ego self-gratifying way of life, but I suppose my soul had other ideas and that is why the angelic messenger came in the dream. Now *Messenger of Love* is one of my favorites. Perhaps I have grown and learned some things about unconditional love."

"You certainly have and still are. That was a very powerful healing dream which helped put you on the path of self-transformation. Your highly intuitive and acute sensitivity make it easy for you to enter many alternate states of consciousness. Those who say that dreams are imaginary fancies are mistaken. There is so much more to dreams than people are aware of. Fortunately, the shamans and medicine healers of your indigenous peoples have much more appreciation, and respect for the many transformational powers of dreams. This book will be a dream journey, but that makes it no less real or not applicable to daily life. In some ways, it will actually be 'more real' than what you experience in your everyday life. You have even begun to invoke your subconscious mind to give you dreams to offer insight, clarity and understanding on various issues and karmic circumstances. That is to be commended and it is my hope that many others will begin doing likewise. For example, that dream state you entered in May of 1984 was a life saver for you."

"I was suicidal at the time. The pain of unrequited love was unbearable. I truly felt that I could not go on. I remember hoping to not wake up in the morning. That was the worst night of my life. It felt like a hammer was pummeling my heart. And like you said, early the next morning something came over me. I woke up at five a.m. and it was like I was in a trance. I took out my notebook and wrote a page, having no idea what I was scribbling so quickly. Then I fell back to sleep. When I awoke, I knew something very powerful had happened. Somehow my agony and deep depression had taken me to a different place or maybe I was going crazy."

"You have to be a little crazy to be on the Earth and in your case, to be an artist. Being a little crazy is a good thing. Yes, you were in bad shape then. Now you can move past all of that. You felt so alone and you still do sometimes, but you are learning and evolving. How my eyes twinkle when I see people clean up their 'bargage', their baggage/garbage, as you coined a new word. You are quite good with words."

"Might you have a little hand in it since I'm sure that you have a sense of humor?"

"I have a sense of a lot of things, and humor is definitely one of them. I like to make you laugh. Heaven only knows you have cried enough."

"A few rivers I suppose and not all have been tears of sorrow."

"You are coming along nicely. I would like for you to include some of your 'writings' in this book, now that you have a nice quiet place where you can write, undisturbed. I had my hand in that as well. You know the saying, 'Watch what you ask for, you will get it.' You uttered a very special, sacred prayer to me back in July of last year. I like to call it your POMP prayer, your Peace of Mind Plea. Plea se, is one of the most powerful and beautiful words in the human language. People are usually more than glad to pass you the bread, butter, or whatever when you say please, or utter a respectful plea. This is why you are wise to teach your children the benefits of frequently using the word please."

"That makes sense. You really are good with words."

"Thank you and how very pleas ed I am to share multiple word meanings with you. There is far more significance to words and their sounds than you realize. Your POMP, peace of mind plea, came from your heart and soul. Those pleas are the ones that make it first to Heaven. You were very sincere about your plea. You were at the end of your rope. That is not always a bad place to be. Sometimes, you have to hit rock bottom before you can climb back up the rope and start a new life."

"I can sure relate to that. Last year was a bad year. I was in a difficult relationship. I visited my family constantly to get away from the fighting and pain."

"I know and one morning you did something you had not done in some time and that is what got my attention. You prayed your POMP prayer. To quote you exactly, you said, 'Dear God, I beg you for peace of mind. My home is not my home anymore. There is nothing but turmoil and conflict here. I feel trapped in this relationship. Please help me.'

"That was your plea. You did not define or demand in what manner help would come. You did something else essential for prayers to be answered. You surrendered! That is a biggie! People pray every day for any number of things. The requests make Santa's list look like a toddler's scribbling. People pray every day, but many lack humility and the desire or ability to surrender. To have the desire to surrender to their own soul, inner strength, higher power (as AA would call it), whatever terms you want to use, is all it takes for spiritual forces to come to your rescue. This is a lesson worth internalizing and why I am sharing this story of your POMP prayer.

"Like I said, I have infinite ways and means to come to your rescue when you offer your pleas e and prayers out of surrender and sincerity. I can take any circumstance or situation and help turn it to your benefit as long as your prayer truly comes from the heart. When you surrender, you are ready to challenge your fears and to make new choices and changes. You create everything. Let me repeat, you create everything and I do mean everything in your life experience based on the Universal Law of Attraction which is such a popular topic these days. Well, I think I have said enough for now and given you some information to think and write about. Now I will take my leave."

"Please don't go," I pleaded. "This is so fascinating. I'm afraid if you leave I'll never see you again. Can you stay and talk to me forever?"

"I most certainly could, but you are not up for that."

"I'm sure glad you came. I do feel different now – somehow better and less depressed."

"Good. This conversation will give you a lot to write about."

"I hope I can remember the things you've said."

"You will. We'll talk again soon. By the way, thanks for a wonderful cup of coffee," Mr. Divine said, then disappeared into thin air.

I immediately awakened. I rubbed my eyes and let out a sigh. "I've been drugged," I wanted to say, but I knew such was not true. I had a strong urge to write, so I turned on the light, took out my notebook and scribbled notes as fast as I could. I would fill in the details later.

Over the next few weeks my emotions alternated between confusion, wonderment, doubt and moments of intense joy and even ecstasy. Part of me felt that something wonderful had happened to me. I had been waiting all my life for something like this to happen. I even had dreams over the years where a divine being visited me, but in those dreams I only saw scattered images and misty pictures. The setting and scenery were always ethereal and surrealistic. Sometimes, I would see orbs of golden light with stars encircling them and I would be filled with wonder and powerful feelings of love. I would try to concentrate and focus so the images would become clearer, but it never worked. I would only awaken with feelings of longing and sadness – always wanting to see and experience more.

As wonderful as it was, my joy was short lived. My critical "left brain monster" as I humorously refer to my logical mind, would not accept that a divine being (Mr. Divine as he calls himself) could visit me in dreams, let alone in person. One of the things I have always been grateful for is that I have a strong critical mind. I don't accept ideas until I have mentally put them through the scrutiny of logical reasoning then assimilated them into my thinking. This involves constant intense analyzing, sorting out and weighing ideas based on previous experiences, debating, and so forth. This I call my left brain work. I always enjoyed debating in high school and college and loved to challenge people's ideas and beliefs. How arrogant it is when people claim to know so much! Even the famous Greek philosopher Socrates said something to the effect that the key to knowledge is in admitting that we know very little. He was known for challenging cocky orators, and he derived much satisfaction from finding loopholes and contradictions in their arguments.

With all that said, how could I possibly dare to claim to know that "divinity" or God could make personal direct contact with me? "Come on now, you have a good brain, now use it!" I could hear my left brain haranguing me. "You made good grades in college in philosophy, theology, and psychology classes because you utilized your logical mind and intelligence, not entertaining mumbo jumbo fantasies. I could just hear the scientists and left brained intellectuals ridiculing me, since I had no empirical proof to claim to have experienced a visit from "the head honcho." At that moment, I wanted empirical proof more than anything in the world. I even imagined asking Mr. Divine to prove to me that the dream was more than fantasy, even though I had to admit, I have always felt that there is more to "fantasy" and "the imagination" than people know or admit.

I feared my left brain cognitive mind might drive me nuts asking so many questions and filling me with doubts and confusion. And yet I also was in constant close contact with my right brain intuitive side which had accepted many experiences over the years from precognitive dreams, clairvoyance to visions of the future. My imagination was very active and awakened as well. I could never logically prove the existence of my imaginary playmates or the characters from my stories; yet I had derived so much consolation and enjoyment from their company.

Needless to say, I was in quite a quandary. After two weeks passed, my doubting and fearful side took over and I started freaking out. Filled with confusion and fright, I saw images of me flipping out and going totally hysterical. Maybe I did need to sign myself into a mental institution and put myself in the hands of a shrink. I confess that such thoughts crossed my mind many times, but I was also well aware that superior intelligence and intellectual brilliance promise no guarantee of sanity. Some of the most brilliant artists and minds of the times succumbed to madness or insanity. I thought of one of my favorite philosophers – Friedrich Nietzsche who fell victim to mental illness. My favorite ballet dancer is the famous Russian Ballet Dancer, Vaslav Nijinsky. After a short, highly successful career as dancer and choreographer, Nijinsky was diagnosed with schizophrenia, then spent many years in and out of psychiatric hospitals and asylums.

Is that where I will wind up if I entertain any more crazy notions? I wondered. Did I need to see a shrink before my delusions and approaching madness worsened? A psychiatrist might have some drugs that could keep such dreams from returning. I wanted nothing to do with this "Mr. Divine" character who claimed to be God. I concluded that he was even crazier than me. How dare he take advantage of my extreme sensitivity and come to me in dreams, knowing that I have excellent dream recall. It just wasn't possible for such contact to take place. I even had more wine than I should have for the next few nights, hoping to numb myself from my dreams. It must have worked because he did not show up. As a matter of fact, I stopped recalling my dreams for awhile. At least I did not have to deal with this Mr. Divine character! So what if my dreams were put on hold for awhile; that was probably for a good reason. I could live without remembering my dreams until I got cured of this ailment of the soul.

Then a strange thing happened. A few days later, I was browsing in a video shop and came upon a recording of a live concert by Bette Midler called Divine Madness. Bette Midler was often called the divine Miss M. during that raucous period of her live show performances. That made me think of my dream and Mr. Divine which I was wondering might be nothing more than a fantasy dream character I had concocted to ease my loneliness and boredom. "Divine madness." I said out loud. I don't think there's anything divine going on here, but there certainly is some madness. I hurried out of the video store and tried to forget about the experience. It did not happen! It seemed the word "divine" popped up everywhere. I attended a Christmas concert with a friend and of course the first soloist sang my favorite carol "O Holy Night." Every time she would sing the phrase "O Night Divine," I'd feel a twitching in my stomach. When she sang the final chorus and went for the high note singing "O night, divine," I thought she was going to hold that "divine" note forever. To make matters worse, after we applauded the performers with a standing ovation, my friend had to say, "Michael, that Christmas concert was simply *divine*." I wanted to throw up.

I tried with all my might and willpower to forget the experience, but I just could not. To my consternation, I found myself missing my dreams and I also missed Mr. Divine. I could not explain it, nor define this longing. I reviewed my notes. The missing continued. How could I miss someone who might be nothing more than a figment of my imagination? I did not have a logical answer for that question anymore than I have logical explanations for any of the characters I meet in my imagination which leads to a story. I was proud that some had even found their way into fantasy and science fiction magazines.

"Yes, but getting a fantasy story published is not the same thing as claiming to talk to 'the head honcho,' my mind countered. My mind had its hey day. I did not sign myself into a mental institution and the more I thought about my divine visitor, the more I missed him. He had said so many wonderful things to me. He was kind and filled me with hope and a sense that there is so much more to life than we experience. I began to challenge my ruthless mind. After all, Mr. Divine had said nothing that was deleterious in any way. On the contrary, everything he said was uplifting, empowering, informative and loving. How could that be bad? Still, my mind wanted to dismiss the experience as illusion. I may struggle with accepting unusual ideas and having my horizons and belief systems stretched, but one thing about me is that I am not one to give up so easily to the whims of my mind or my emotions. One may dominate for awhile, but the other always comes around. I reminded my logical side that Mr. Divine had said nor done nothing to upset, scare or put me in any kind of danger. On the contrary, he had shown kindness, and expressed words that were interesting, thought provoking, comforting and wise. I have always believed in stretching our horizons. The next few weeks were going to see my horizons and beliefs stretched tremendously, and as my divine guest predicted and promised, I did not go over the edge or have a mental collapse.

I decided to have an open mind and heart. I would be receptive to the unknown and see what I could learn from it. My imagination had never abandoned or let me down before. I would give it a chance to sail with me on even more exotic journeys on the seas of the psyche. I promised myself that when doubts start to assail me, I would quote one of my favorite people, Albert Einstein, who said, "Imagination is more important than knowledge."

So yes, in that wonderful dream world I shared my first cup of coffee that very morning with the king of kings, the Divine Almighty. I stepped into a world of wonderment that became so entrenched in my soul that the memories of those shared mornings turned my life completely around. They gave me answers that I thought not possible and took away my fear of growing old. My journey in life is now just that, a journey, not a chore or drudgery. I truly understand light and love and peace. It is time to lose the selfishness of keeping this to myself. It is time to relive those endearing talks with him and share them with you!

Chapter Two

I come to you with Great Knowing!

"Mr. Divine, please visit me again." I prayed the next night. The following Monday I had the distinct feeling that he was going to visit me in the morning. How did I know? I don't know; I just did. Promptly the next day, I experienced my second dream visit with Mr. Divine. I was asleep, but I was also observing myself, like in a lucid dream. This was not the first time I had experienced lucid dreaming. Lucid dreams especially grab my attention because it feels like you are filming your own movie or writing your own novel, while at the same time observing yourself doing that very thing. Lucid dreaming has become a popular subject over the years and there are many fine books about the topic.

Back to the dream. I am putting out two coffee mugs on the table, choosing two cupid mugs that had been a Valentine's gift some years ago. I had never used them; this would be the perfect occasion. I looked in the freezer and saw two bags: I took a whiff of Hazlenut cream and Dark French Roast and chose the latter and filled up the coffee-maker.

I glanced at his mug; there were little red heart designs hanging above the heads of cherubs. I looked at the mugs again, then got up to pour myself a cup of coffee. When I turned around, my steaming mug of coffee in hand, there he stood a few feet away. This time his long, golden shimmery, blond hair was pulled back in a pony tail. His face had become even more striking and handsome than the first time we met. He truly looked like a Greek god, with a perfectly chiseled face and bone structure. His physique was sleek and taut. There was this glow about him; could I be seeing his aura? If the halos and auras of saints glow, then why wouldn't Mr. Divine's? On the other hand, maybe the "glow" was nothing more than my eyes playing tricks on me or maybe the glow is what I saw because that is what I wanted or expected to see. The truth of the matter was that although he certainly looked out of the ordinary, he did not dress out of the ordinary. He was wearing tan denim jeans with a navy blue flannel shirt, the top two buttons unbuttoned. He wore two small silver star earrings in both ears. I wanted to ask him if he was keeping up with current tastes and trends, but remained silent. He gave me a little nod which made me feel that he was reading my thoughts and then he sat down. This time there were no clinking noises when I poured Mr. Divine his cup of coffee.

Very little was said during the first cup. Needless to say, I was thrilled when he asked for a second cup. He took a few sips and looked at me lovingly. How very human he looked and that warmed my heart as the hot mug warmed my hands, taking away the bite off the morning chill. I sipped my coffee quietly at the table and looked at him, a little less nervous than last time. We were both silent a few minutes. The only sound was our sipping as we drank our coffee. I had been meditating for a few years and have come to love the silence, so I am comfortable spending time alone. My thoughts wandered a little longer, then I took my last sip of coffee and gently laid my cup down. I looked at Mr. Divine, feeling kind of nervous. Had he been aware of my internal predicament over the past few weeks and was that why he had stayed away? As though reading my thoughts, he smiled then began speaking softly.

"I come to you with Great Knowing! I invite you to partake of many treasures I have to offer. I invite you to visit lovely places of beauty. I would like you to visit people in the places your soul beckons you. I invite you to listen and learn from them, to share stories together, and to celebrate your humanity. I invite you to meet me at the portal of inner worlds where the threshold of imagination bridges matter and spirit. There we will have fellowship. Michael, cultivate your will and intention to visit a certain place and watch your desire joyously manifest for you. Did you not have a lovely vacation in Florida last January? You slipped out of your limited human thinking and let your awareness and imagination soar to the realm of your most prized dreams. You challenged your limited thinking and beliefs. You told yourself, 'I have only been to Disney World once in my life. Wouldn't it be nice to go?' a voice whispered in your mind."

"Yes, I will go back there someday," I told myself.

"The thought was placed in your mind that in reality there is no time. This world can be your playground. You have only to believe with the faith of a child and I shall bestow a gift unto you much the way Santa spoils you at Christmas. And why can't I spoil you? Soon your dream to go to Disney world began to take shape and form in your mind. You fed it with energy and enthusiasm from your potent imagination. Soon you were imagining you were at Disney World having a grand time. You imagined Florida's golden sun rays warming you. You tasted the fluffy cotton candy, and waved at Mickey and Minnie Mouse and other Disney characters strolling about. The dream gathers momentum each time you think about it; this allows the dream to draw itself towards you like a magnet via 'the universal law of attraction'. You step into the eternal present as you realize that the future is only as far away as you imagine. You imagine it closer, moving in towards you; drawing closer to you because you want to be in Florida now. Not later. Not someday. Right now.

"The stretching of your imagination allowed the doors of opportunity to open. You heard from a friend a few days later who told you of a spiritual Expo that was taking place in Orlando, Florida in mid-January, just some six weeks away. Coincidence some say. Not you. There was an opening for spiritual readers at the Expo. You signed up. A few weeks later you were off to sunny Florida for the first time in twenty-six years. You went because you believed you could go. The trip manifested because you believed it could. I am here to help you believe and manifest the true desires of your heart.

"In the yearnings are the seeds of fulfillment. Believe and be filled to the brim. I wish that every day be as Christmas for each and every one of you. It is as easy as you see and believe. Step beyond time and see 'good times' and 'good things' in your mind and imagination. I can help make your sojourn here on Earth a

most pleasant journey of countless adventures, and joyous
tomorrows whose memories you can relish for many years."

Mr. Divine suddenly became quiet. His eyes looked distant.
He smiled at me, then his head bent slightly and he drifted off.
A few minutes later he woke up. He looked at me with such
kindness and compassion, then he spoke softly. "Michael, I have
always been real to you. This you have sensed most of your life.
You have always believed in 'your invisible friends'. Even when
your friends would tell you they were only make-believe, you
would tell yourself that they were real. They *are* real as I am real.
Even during the times you tried to shun me and dismiss me, there
was always a little voice telling you that I am real. Those times
you felt my presence were not dreams or imaginary wanderings."

"I remember very well. I'd tell myself to stop lest someone
hear me and think me nuts. It never worked, but I did halfway
convince myself that I was just a lonely boy making it all up."

"Halfway is a good word. You could never convince
yourself completely because you have always known in your soul
that I am always with you. Remember that painting of Jesus that
hung above your bed in your foster home near your sister?"

"Yes, that was a most striking picture of Jesus. It looked so
real. Every time I looked at it, I felt powerful emotions and
tingles went all through me. The more I'd look at it, the dreamier
and more light headed I became. My initial feeling was that
Jesus was looking at me from the eyes of that painting, but like
always, I dismissed the feeling. I would get cold chills every time
I looked at that painting. I could stand in front of it and get lost.
Time would stop and I'd be filled with longings and yearnings I
could not understand, let alone explain."

"You wanted to be with me, Michael. I remember a couple
of times when you prayed. While looking at the painting, you
said, 'Dear, God please take me with you. This world is not my
home. I am not happy here. There is nothing here for me.'"

"I did say those words. That was so long ago."

"Let me tell you a little secret. It was not Jesus who was
looking at you from the eyes of that painting – it was me."

"Oh my goodness," I exclaimed. "To think that I got so scared that I took the painting down and put it under the bed."

"I can understand how you felt and how the experience frightened you. Yet I also understand how you always went back to it. Something compelled you back. I should say 'someone' compelled you back. If you search deep in your memories, you will recall that a few times you thought you saw the eyes move. You would blink and close your eyes, thinking you were imagining things. Even though you put the painting away, it was not long before you went back to it and hung it back on the wall."

"I'd get frightened and take it down, then I'd miss it and hang it up again. If I had told my foster mother, she'd probably have thought I was a nut case. Fortunately, she never came in my room. I have to admit that part of me derived much comfort from the painting."

"That is because on deeper levels, I was very real to you then; it is sad that you had nobody to talk to. Michael, I was very real to you then during your difficult years in the foster homes as I am here right now. You were not ready at that time for a visit such as this. Now you are. Your sadness and loneliness have shown and taught you much about love. They have helped lead you to love's sacred portals. I want you to know that you are capable of loving deeply and intimately."

"I've always sensed that and I think it scares me and makes me try to shut myself off emotionally as deeply as I yearn for friendship. For years, I could not look people in the eye, and I'd get nervous when someone looked at me, especially men."

"I know," he said softly. "The eyes are the window of the soul as the saying goes and you can sense things about people when you look into their eyes."

"My father used to stare at me. He could be the most devious, cruel and manipulative person I ever knew. He'd look at me a certain way and I thought that the devil or pure evil was looking at me."

"Unfortunately, your father is a very tortured, troubled soul, very 'touched and tainted by the darkness' as the saying goes. Sadly, he brought along many demons from past lives and his skeletons in the closet created many hardships and difficulties for your family."

"I used to say he had 'the evil eye.'"

"Your father was never 'pure evil,' but his darkness went very deep. His cruelties were partially the result of the influences and encouragement he received subconsciously from devious entities and spirits who have been following him over the course of many past lives. That is what happens when a soul does not confront their inner darkness, challenge and transform it into light. You cannot be healed as long as you avoid or deny the darkness that dwells within. There comes a point when everyone must face their darkness, confront and move through it."

"That's been a lifetime journey for me."

"You have come so far and many are very proud of you, including me."

"Thank you. I like to think I have faced many of my inner demons; yet I'm sure there are more."

"There are, and for each one you face and deal with, each additional confrontation becomes less difficult. For as you heal, so does your soul light brighten and your darkness wanes. If only people would realize the need to face and confront their inner demons and darkness."

"I can certainly see the temptation not to. Many times I thought facing and acknowledging my darkness would destroy me; it just got to be too much at times."

"I know, but you knew on a deeper level that facing your darkness would not destroy you; it would heal you. There were just a few times that you went overboard and bit off more than you could chew. Facing the darkness is a difficult journey that must be taken with much care, respect and caution. You are awakening and activating many intense subconscious energies and bringing up powerful forces that must be released. This process must not be rushed or it can lead to disaster. It can drive a person mad."

"Maybe that's why my father would never deal with his inner demons. Not only did he *not* acknowledge or face them, he denied them. I have learned that to repress and deny the darkness is very dangerous."

"Your father is a good example of that. He had much inner rage against his mother that he never dealt with. Your poor mother bore the brunt of his violent explosions due to rage at women, namely his mother."

"For years I hated him, but I denied it. Finally, I came to realize that I had to admit that hatred and deal with it if I ever wanted to heal and move through it. I, like many others, spent years trying to run from my darkness. I think that's why I had so many nightmares of demons and monsters chasing me in the dark. I would wake up breathing hard and be drenched in sweat from all that running. I was also petrified of the dark for years. I even wrote a poem in the eighth grade that began with the line 'Why do I fear the darkness when it does not fear me?' A therapist helped me realize that those dreams were showing me I needed to stop running and to start facing my darkness. It was no easy task to undertake. Nonetheless, I began a very arduous and long journey of healing. I had a lot of hollering to get through in therapy as part of that healing.

"It's not over yet. It was years before I could look at people without getting nervous and could enjoy it when they looked at me. For years it was torture looking into a mirror. I was such a mess then. Kahlil Gibran in *The Prophet* said, 'Your joy is your sorrow unmasked. The deeper that sorrow carves into your being, the more joy you can contain.'"

"Gibran is a very wise man. When sorrow heals, it is transmuted into wisdom and if you will allow me to pay you a compliment, you are a bit of a wise man yourself, Michael."

"Thank you, Mr. Divine. You make me blush. I've certainly had enough sorrow in this lifetime."

"I think you will concur that now it is time for more joy in your life. You are becoming more excited about life again for both yourself and for others. We are drinking the best morning coffee one could imagine. It feels so delicious going down the throat that we sigh in joyous delight. Your sorrowful yesterdays are transforming into joyous todays and tomorrows, and you are discovering, much to your ever increasing satisfaction, that I am rooting for you. I am committed to helping you realize your dreams as I have helped inspire many of your writings.

"For many years, writing has been a creative outlet to help you to explore your inner self – both the light and the dark. The light of your soul holds many treasures, but always remember that despair and pain are very powerful and sacred teachers and hold their own treasures and gifts. The dawn is preceded by the darkest moments of night. Your dark nights of the soul precede many of your creative breakthroughs in writing. Your yearnings, pain, and suffering have led you to the path of wisdom. Just as a mother experiences pain when giving birth to her baby, so have you experienced much pain which has led to the birth of your creative writing; which I might add has sustained you for over twenty years."

"Don't give me too much credit. For years I didn't even think about or recall having written those inspirational things. Sometimes I figure why bother writing at all."

"It is true, that which is said has already been said before, and yet each time it is said again, it is new and fresh. That which you have said before, you will say again in fresh words, ideas and images. Everything is new and yet it is not. Everything has been said and yet it has not been said."

"That makes sense. So many times in the past I have put away my writing only to go back to it weeks or months later to get all excited and passionate again. Then after awhile, the flames of enthusiasm begin to wane, and before you know it, I am not writing anymore."

"The past is spilled milk as the saying goes. Start writing again and see how much better you begin to feel."

"That always happens. I have to admit though, that sometimes I doubt the truth of anything I write."

"Do not be harsh on the doubting part of you, but don't overindulge it either. Most of your doubts come from deeply ingrained beliefs which have been instilled in you from worn out ideologies and doctrines. Such false doctrines were created to control people. I am here to tell you that everyone has invisible friends and mentors or a muse as you like to refer to the spirit of your inspiration. How much happier will your world be when everyone embraces their muse with open arms."

"Well, even if I'm making this dream up, I have to admit I feel better to hear you tell me how important my writing is."

"It *is* very important and you need to make time to write. Let yourself be absorbed and transformed by the dynamic process of creation. Think of how empty and sad the world would be without music, poetry, and art. Be glad to be among the artists, for such is your soul's calling. It is an honor to be an artist even if your culture does not value art as it should."

"Baseball and other sports celebrities earn far more than most artists."

"Don't let that discourage you. There is good news. There will come a time in your evolution when your artists will receive the honor, respect, and attention they merit. More of your artists are proudly accepting who they are. As they make daily efforts towards expressing their inner self, many are receiving telepathic inspirations from souls on such evolved worlds as Venus and other star systems such as Sirius, the Pleaides, and Arcturus. These evolved star brethren and sisters shall truly be your spearheads who shall teach you the 'Joyous Art of Living'."

I lit up at the mention of Venus. "Can you talk more about Venus?"

"Yes I will, but not today. We will save your 'Venus adventures' for next time."

"I can hardly wait."

"I will say that some muses do come from Venus and other places where art and love are experienced in ways far more beautiful and intense than you experience on the Earth. When you wrote *Venusian Meditation,* you were tapping into Venusian energy."

"Words often pop in my mind out of nowhere. When I sensed that I was making some mental Venusian contact, I told myself that such could not be the case and I had to be making it up."

"If it is any comfort, you were not making it up. On the more evolved worlds such as Venus (there are many more; some far more evolved than Venus), communication is telepathic. Even now you sometimes telepathically sense what people are thinking before they speak. This is an unconscious skill you and many old souls possess. Words are limited forms of expression and communication, and in time when humanity further evolves, the spoken word will become obsolete.

"This is, by the way, why some people are accused of not being good listeners. They sense and often know what the other person is going to communicate before or shortly after they begin speaking. They only need a few verbal cues and words before they comprehend the gist of what the person is endeavoring to convey. Some people can observe body language or even look at the person and know what they are thinking. This happens more than you might think."

"My friend Victoria used to get annoyed with me for interrupting her so much."

"It is not that you were trying to be rude, you just often grasped what she was communicating before she finished her sentences. It was tedious and frustrating to hear her repeat what you already had comprehended. But you must be more patient. Even when you can sense what others are about to say, you must allow them to voice their thoughts. Their minds are not operating at the speed yours is. Ask your muse to slow down when ideas pour too fast into your mind. Above all, please continue making time for your writing. I predict that you are going to fall in love with your writing and your muse all over again and I predict publication success as well."

"Oh, goodness, there it is, that 'fall in love' phrase again that makes me uncomfortable."

"It is time for love to make you comfortable, Michael. To fall in anything is to become vulnerable. You do not know where you are going to land or even if you are going to land anywhere at all. There is uncertainty involved. You must take risks if you want to fully experience life. Well, I think we've had enough for one day. I want you to spend some time getting reacquainted with your writings that you have written over the years. We'll talk again soon."

Chapter Three

Venusian Meditation

I was higher than a kite for the rest of the day. That Mr. Divine predicted publication success was icing on the cake. *So what that it was just a dream, whatever that means,* my thoughts rambled. In my heart, I knew these were not just ordinary dreams to be taken lightly. Mr. Divine and I were involved in business most serious and sacred, I might add. I was feeling more and more inspired to get back to my writing. That alone was reason enough for further contact with Mr. Divine.

I took notes for the following several days. Every time I would think I had recalled everything, something else would pop in my head and I had to write it down. Along with a new joy that was beginning to stir in the depths of my being, my mind did its usual analyzing. I knew I'd be hearing the protests and mental babblings for days to come, but I didn't care. This visit had been wonderful. Mr. Divine certainly knows the way to my heart – it is through my art. My writing is my one true undeniable passion.

I dug out Venusian Meditation and read it along with other things I had written so long ago. I found it so interesting that Mr. Divine spoke about my attraction and connection to Venus. He seemed to know everything about me and he brought up that painting of Jesus that had intrigued, fascinated, and haunted me for years. "Well, if he's the 'head honcho,' I suppose he should know everything about everybody," I said out loud with a big grin on my face. I had been puzzled about that painting for years and thought about it many times after I left the foster home. To hear Mr. Divine speak about it gave the experience more meaning. He predicted that I'd fall in love again with my writing and my muse. That in itself, is reason enough to justify the visits, I told my doubting mind. I always feel better when I write. It was nice to be reminded of that because the writing struggle has been with me most of my life. Maybe I would get back on the ball and put in time every day. Maybe I'd even get some books published. The thought sparked a little flame of hope in me. "Mr. Divine, you are heaven sent," I said to him that night in my prayers. "Please come back soon!"

Two days later we had our third visit. I was feeling kind of perky and bouncy and was humming as I made my way downstairs. There he sat at the kitchen table dressed in a red jogging suit and white sneakers with his long glistening hair hanging down his shoulders. I wondered if he was dressed this way because I have been an avid jogger for years. He poured us both a cup of steaming French Vanilla Coffee. We were quiet a few moments. The silence was welcome. I have always been puzzled as to why most people think you have to be constantly talking if you are with someone. Are people uncomfortable with the silence? I often wondered.

It was the silence that had led me to my rich inner world and imagination. Sometimes talk was just too much, and for years I probably talked twice or three times more than most people. To go from nonstop constant babbling to needing frequent meditation and silence was some ninety degree turn. I heard a word from my writing, *Look Not Away*, "People talk when they have forgotten who they are. They avoid eye contact if you look for their soul behind their faint smiles." I now believe that I talked so much because I was afraid I might actually hear the voice of my own soul. I kept myself constantly distracted with noise and talking as a means to numb depression and anxiety at the cost of drowning out the voice of my soul.

I looked at Mr. Divine. He nodded as though acknowledging and agreeing with my silent words. Then he spoke gently, "So you want to know about your connection to Venus?"

I lit up. "Oh, yes please!"

"Let me begin by saying that you are not confined or limited to your physical lifetimes on the Earth, and there are many nuances of what constitutes physical."

"Are you telling me that we have lives on other planets and on other universes as well?"

"Yes, but don't look surprised. You have been drawn to Venus for a long time."

"I know, but I thought that was just because I love reading about Venus in mythology."

"Mythology, along with fantasy and science fiction provide a useful framework for many truths. People accept truth on the levels they are capable. Some can only accept truth at intellectual rational levels. Others go further and are daring and brave enough to accept as real some of the experiences and truths of their inner worlds that others relegate to the domain of mythology, the imagination and fantasy. To begin, I'd like for you to share your experiences with Venus. Let yourself and your readers determine for themselves if they consider them truth or fantasy."

"Well, I have always been drawn to Venus. When we learned about the other planets in our solar system in science class in school, our teacher asked us which planet we would visit if given the opportunity. I said Venus. The boys made fun of me saying that Venus, the so-called planet of love, was for sissies and sentimental girls. They would choose the war like planet of Mars. A few years later I went to a hypnosis demonstration. The hypnotist had us take some deep breaths and she began counting. The only thing I can recall her saying is that, "You are now going on a journey to a very sacred and beautiful place." Then I was gone. I could feel myself floating, or some part of me because another part of me was aware of Charlie the gray cat, who was scampering about. The next thing I knew, I was standing on the shores of Venus beholding beautiful temples fashioned in all manners of lovely dome designs and constructs I had never seen before. I could hear music that made tears come to my eyes; even the air was perfumed in some exquisite fragrance that a rose can only faintly compare to.

"It felt like my feet were going to float off the ground; I was about to head to one of the temples when the facilitator began speaking softly and brought us back from our journey. I tried to go back in my meditations, but never was able. One day, some years later when I was depressed, I put on some soft music and

entered a meditative state. I felt light headed. Everything was
not as clear as it was during the hypnosis experience, but I could
feel some of the sweetness and the air around me seemed to take
on some of that lovely fragrance again. When the music stopped,
I could feel myself descending, much the same way I felt myself
descending when the hypnotist brought us back. I remember
thinking I have to go back up. 'I have to go back up there,' I said
softly. Then I added. 'That is where I belong. That is my home.'

"I got up slowly and tried to make sense of my surroundings.
I closed my eyes, blinking them several times in hopes I could go
back to that lovely place on Venus. Finally, it dawned on me that
I was no longer there. Uncertain as to whether the experience
was only a dream or a fantasy, I was drawn to get my pencil and
notebook and I wrote *Venusian Meditation*." It's one that I have
memorized."

"May we hear it now, Michael?"

"Gladly."

Venusian Meditation

Yonder lies a world beyond your highest dreams where
yesterday, today, and tomorrow merge as one. Sadness and pain
may not enter this shore. Here, love, peace and happiness prevail.
When you were born, a part of you died. When you die again
shall you be born. Oh, body, how you imprison my soul. How I
long for the day you set me free.

I close my eyes to this world and glimpse past the setting sun
to behold Venusian sparkling crystal seas of sapphire blue. Then
I gaze into the distance and view an emerald green forest whose
beauty surpasses all earthly sights. Celestial music of Venusian
spheres can be heard by all who close their ears to the sounds of
this world where mortals reign. "Welcome to our world, gentle
soul," speaks a soft voice to my heart. You may visit our land
when you please.

"This land is your home. The serene inner world is real. The
outer world where you live is but a dream. Make quiet time to be
with your soul.

Be escorted to Venusian blissful shores. Meditate in the silence and be enfolded by love. Let your soul be filled with peace once more."

By now I felt ready to board a star ship and head straight to Venus. Mr. Divine encouraged me to share my other Venusian experiences.

"In the Fall of 2001, I was giving a class called 'Past Life Exploration' at a spiritual Center in Fairborn, Ohio. I always do my classes from what I call trance or altered awareness. I cannot explain or define what exactly happens. For lack of a term, I will refer to it as channeling. I usually know beforehand which entity I am going to be bringing through because the hostess will request to hear from someone such as The Blessed Mother Mary, Kuan Yin, St. Francis, Mary Magdalene, Nostradamus, etc.

"I always meditate before each class. After a few minutes in the silence and breathing in the fresh autumn breeze wafting through the window, I heard a soft voice in my mind say, 'I am Vilura of Venus. I would like to assist you in your class if that is agreeable to you.' I jerked a little, a bit startled as I had never felt this presence before. I was once more filled with the peace and serenity I had felt during the hypnosis experience and when I wrote *Venusian Meditation.*

"We did our introductions and had a meditation and we invited our angels and guides to join us. We chanted a few om's and sang *This Little Light of Mine.* For the next two hours Vilura of Venus talked about things I knew little or nothing about. People were crying, laughing, joking, and everyone wanted a tape of the class. The next day I was booked for readings. That evening my hostess prepared a lovely dinner of baked salmon, potatoes, home grown green beans, and a lovely salad with freshly baked bread. She, her husband, and I enjoyed each other's company and the lovely meal on the back porch veranda. Then Ron went inside to make some phone calls. Marie and I sipped wine and nibbled on a French pastry and chatted. A time later she reached for my hand and we went to the basement where classes and healings are held. She led me to a bookcase and took a book from the shelf. I was immediately drawn to the portrait of the lovely blue eyed fair woman on the book cover. I was so captivated that I did not even notice the words of the title printed in light pink.

Marie, handed me the book and said, "Michael, I want you to have this book. I have kept it until I knew who it was intended for. It's for you. A gift from me to you," she said in French, kissing me on the cheeks as the French are noted for.

"Thank you," I whispered, "I don't know what to say."

"Merci, suffit," she whispered, (thank you will suffice). "Enjoy it! I'm retiring for the night now. If you need anything, just let me know."

I took the book to the beautiful guest room, all done in light blue and white, and opened it and read for awhile. It was about a Venusian walk-in, a woman who began her life on Venus, but came to complete it on the Earth after switching bodies with a human woman who wanted to die. I was so lost in the story that I again forgot to look at its title. It was only after my eyes began getting drowsy that I put the book down on the night table and crawled beneath the covers. I took one more look at the book. It was titled *From Venus I came*."

Mr. Divine had a big grin on his face. He spoke softly. "What a fascinating story. Have you any more Venus stories?"

"I do have one more. A friend and I went to a Psychic Festival in Ottawa, Canada about three years ago. Sitting across our booth was a trance channeler who had done sessions for Shirley MaClaine. There were several pictures of him sitting beside the acclaimed movie star and New Age matriarch as some call her. We signed up for readings early before he got busy. I was immediately taken in by the man. With eyes closed, and his hands moving about in gestures as he spoke, his Scottish accent charmed me instantly. He spoke of several issues in my life and gave good sound advice. When the time was nearly up, he asked if I had a final question. I asked if he knew of my origins before I came to the Earth. As though I had asked him about the weather, he nonchalantly said, 'My dear lad, you came to the Earth by way of Venus.' My mouth dropped. 'I could hear those words in my mind for weeks. So tell me, have I been there before or not?'"

"Yes, you have and more than once. Venusians have made the transition from the third to the fourth dimensional frequency. They are in possession of light ethereal bodies which are invisible to human sight and telescopes. They possess the ability to block anyone from seeing or perceiving them whose intentions are not in harmony with their own. Since you have forgotten much of what your soul knows to be true, now you have to rely upon your soul vision to move your consciousness through space to that lovely world that has more than once been your home."

"I can see it now, me the big laugh of every psychiatrist, and read their journal headlines 'Deluded man claims to have had past lives on the planet Venus, and goes back for visits under hypnosis.' I'm sure they'd love to probe my crazy mind."

"In many cases, the so-called crazy person is far less crazy than those who label them as crazy."

"I know, but you have to admit it, having such thoughts and experiences can cause you to doubt if you are playing with a full deck."

"Your mind loves to doubt. When in doubt, listen to your heart. In how many stories is this theme central?"

"Quite a few. I read in some book that love is so intense on Venus that souls will often head to Mars after a lifetime there; they simply cannot take in that much love."

"Can you take in that much love?"

"I think that part of me can. I told a friend many years ago that if I let my guard down, I would fall in love with everyone; so yes I am aware of the part of me that can love everyone in ways that transcend human love. I even feel love for plants and animals."

"You experienced some of that love in your Franciscan monk life. Part of you fears to let such deep love fill you again. Yet your soul knows that 'a full and great complete love' is the only kind of love that will bring you true happiness. Anything less is a compromise and a denial of who you really are. Your true essence is pure love. Since your essence is love, how can your love not be colossal and grand?"

"To think I can experience such love and also be filled with rage is downright frightening."

"Rage is distorted energy encased by fear needing to be transmuted to love. The essence of all energy is love. Part of the healing process involves learning the origins of your anger. Then you learn to weep and grieve your losses and hurts. Shedding tears and expressing anger and grief are very essential to the healing process. How burdensome it is to the soul when one shuts themselves off and closes their hearts to the point that they can no longer express their pain through weeping. You have traveled this road, but you chose to get back in touch with your feelings – both painful and joyous."

"I watched the film *The Color Purple* eight times. The final scene when Celie is reunited with her sister and with her birth children given up for adoption, makes me break down and cry. I had not been able to cry for so long."

"When people are ready to be healed, they attract all the help they could possibly need. Their reward is a total saturation of love."

"That, I confess, also frightens me."

"There is no rush. Healing and integration take time, and you have all the time in the world since time does not exist. All that matters is that you intend to heal and let in the complete and great full love that is the essence of who you truly are. You do not have to rush the process."

"Perhaps to know such a great love might drive me mad. I just don't know if there is room on the Earth for the love you speak of."

"There is certainly room enough and then some. When in doubt, simply read the stories of people who were so filled with an outpouring of love that they saw divinity and loved everyone and everything they beheld. Mother Teresa. Gandhi. Jesus. Teresa de Avila. St. John of the Cross. St. Francis and other mystics have been filled with this complete and great full love. Art and beauty attempt to portray this love. You yourself felt this love in your last life as a French model and painter a few times, but it so frightened you that you shunned it. "

"What a torturous life that was. I was put down and misunderstood. In my regressions I learned that I renounced my art and died very bitter."

"That was a very sad life, and some of your anger stems from the conflicts and unhealed hurts from that life. But look at the progress you have made. As long as you are making efforts to heal, then you are evolving. How much you grow and evolve in this lifetime determines the circumstances, experiences, and people you will attract in your next lifetime. The good news is that this could very well be your last life on the Earth."

"But what about the dreams and visions I've had of me as an opera singer in Sweden? I've even seen the date of my debut at the royal Swedish opera house. It's 2063."

"That is a probable lifetime that you may or may not choose to experience on the Earth."

"Really? It kind of surprises me to hear you say that. I thought I was going to sing opera in my next life. I even know the name I will have."

"You have free will. Before this life ends, your desire to be an opera star may no longer be a priority to you."

"That somehow makes sense. Maybe I could sing on a higher plane and not bother to come back to this Earth."

"You might very well earn that privilege. And on that note, I will take my leave now."

Chapter Four

Beyond Memory, Soul Communion, Soul Journey

Mr. Divine so inspired me that I began digging through my boxes and located more writings. I found my little self-published book, *Soul Murmurs*. My eyes were drawn to three short pieces: *Beyond Memory, Soul Communion, and Soul Journey.* It had been so long since I read them. I remembered the inspiration that filled me during that fertile, creative writing period. How could I have put these writings on shelves to gather dust? Would I ever be able to fully embrace my art?

The next morning Mr. Divine showed up bright and early. I was very happy to hear from him, since after all, he predicted that I'd fall in love with my art and muse again and that gave me some hope I had not felt in some time. After a cup of steaming Hazelnut coffee, he began speaking gently.

"Try not to be discouraged, Michael. There is quite a plethora of mental stirrings going on in your mind. It is sad when people allow the mind to go stagnant and it is refreshing to observe those who constantly keep the mind stimulated. The mind, like muscles, needs to constantly be stimulated and exercised lest lethargy and atrophy set in. There is quite a myriad flurry of activity that goes on in your conscious and subconscious mind. It can be quite a labyrinth in there."

"I'm sure the shrinks would have a heyday getting inside my head and probing around. Maybe I ought to let one hypnotize me."

"That could prove to be an interesting experience."

"I know from high school experiences and the one with the mentalist, Kreskin, that I go under very easily."

"Actually there are many different kinds of hypnosis. Anytime you are tapping the deeper levels of your psyche and accessing greater creativity, you are hypnotizing yourself and opening up to other levels of awareness. The imagination is one of the primary and best tools to help you explore the inner worlds. That is precisely what your science fiction and fantasy novelists do."

"The inner worlds seem so real."

"On other planes, they are very real. Our visits are not third dimensional, but that makes them no less real or valid."

"I must admit how much I am starting to enjoy these visits. They remind me how light-headed and good I feel when I lose myself in my writing. Time seems to stop. Just recently I dug out some essays and could not believe that I had written them. The words flowed so effortlessly."

"Those 'writings' sustained you during times of doubting and questioning. They were often the tiny embers that kept the fires of hope and inspiration from going out. Don't they deserve to be shared?"

"I have to confess, that part of me has always been very hard on myself when it comes to my writings. Though the words just pour, there is always that part of me that judges and criticizes my writings, calling them metaphysical and philosophical fluff, or mumbo jumbo that has nothing to do with everyday life."

"Yes, the inner saboteur can be ruthless in his attacks and criticisms. He not only attacks you when you write the spiritual fluff as you call it; he makes fun of everything you write. Let me see if I got his number down pat. Your poetry is mushy, useless babblings, your short stories and fantasy novel unrealistic garbage, your songs mediocre, mushy, sentimental ramblings of words that make little sense. Do I have him sized up right?"

"Yes."

"Yeah he's a real meanie."

"My therapist was right when she told me that I could never become successful or bond with my writing until I did battle with this part of myself."

"Fortunately, your inner saboteur is not the only character or sub-personality you possess. Those three 'writings' I wish for you to share come from one of your sub-personalities who is very wise. I will take my leave now, but I would like for you to reread those writings today. We will talk about them next time."

"Thanks for your encouragement."

"The pleasure is mine," he said, then disappeared. I woke up a half hour later. A dog was barking in the distance. Moonlight crept in my window. A breeze created a chill in the air. I slowly dragged myself out of bed and got dressed. I recalled the dream very vividly and I immediately took some notes. I lazily sipped my hot chocolate over breakfast and thought about what we discussed. Then I went for a walk. I thought about my writings – many I had forgotten I ever wrote. How long had it been since I last read *Soul Murmurs* or sent the writings out to publishers? Mr. Divine was right. I needed to share my "writings." I ran a few errands, but the thought that I needed to read those writings never left my mind. After a light lunch, I poured myself a diet coke then got comfortable in my big chair. I picked up a booklet *Soul Murmurs* from the table and read.

Beyond Memory

It seems there was a time when I knew everything – the reasons behind the reasons we accept in response to the questions that life poses. As a river flows into the ocean, and the ocean extends itself to embrace and unite with the river, so was at one time my soul united with the infinite All That Is. The infinite flowed through my mortal being, and rejuvenated my soul daily with the nectar of transcendental knowledge.

The deep hunger in my heart to know and understand did not gnaw at my mind and soul, for my mind, heart and soul were as one. I had not tasted from the cup of forgetfulness. I was not haunted by the inner yearnings and vague memories which I cannot define nor grasp; yet whose misty translucent forms never cease to appear before my eyes, disturbing my thoughts.

Unable to clearly see these forms, still I cannot eradicate them. Can I only see their true form in dreams? Can I remember the birth of these memories? Can I return to the place beyond time where memory and knowledge were inseparable? What caused this breach? Is it important or does this breach not exist? Perhaps forgetfulness is a game of the self engaging the self.

In the silence, I hear a faint voice which utters, "Close your eyes. Look inside and you will see beyond the veil of forgetfulness. In reality, there is no time when you did not know everything. Forget no more! Remember and be at peace!"

Soul Communion

I listened to the inner voice who spoke words of truth. It bade me to heed its calling to carry out a difficult task which would transform my life. It asked me to believe in hopes and dreams, and to relinquish my hold on the ropes of attachment which pull one ever so far from the soul's destiny.

The Inner Voice reminded me of my calling to assist in the awakening of others from their slumber so they too might hear the voice of their soul and heed its calling.

"Look about and listen," it said. "The lonely voices of humanity cry forth into the night longing for comfort and peace of heart. Weary souls, chasing mortal delights, are not finding satisfaction. The seductive enticements of Maya ensnare souls, imprisoning them in desire's dark pit where she sucks away their innocence.

"Be strong and valiant," the voice said. "Know that you are a child of the All That Is. Delusion and fear cannot touch you when you remember your true identity. It is time to claim your rightful heritage. You are entitled to peace, joy and bliss. The woes of the world need not tilt your equilibrium. You only participate in pain and sorrow when your consciousness descends to their realm. No one need drink from the bitter cup of sorrow. You have access to everything. There is no place for grief or loss when your attention is centered on your true being. You are a part of everything. How can you lack anything?

"Mortal life is but a temporary diversion for the soul, each life being merely a moment in eternity. The spark of life which opens the newborn's eyes is the same spark which creates and destroys worlds."

The voice assured me that confusion was temporary and would fade as the rays of transcendental knowledge shone forth, illuminating my perceptions and vision.

My soul rejoiced that I listened to the words it uttered. I do look forward to the quiet moments of tomorrow when my soul and I will commune once more!

Soul Journey

The roads are many to the celestial fields of paradise where peace and bliss dwell. All souls make this long journey, meeting the grand foe of fear who diverts their attention, knowing it can only delay the journey every soul is destined to complete.

All travel the road to mediocrity; some for days or months, others for years or lifetimes. The detours of this road are many – each mile leading to thicker more obscure roads which further alienate the self from the self. This road leads to no destination. It only wears down the body and soul. All travelers on this crooked path eventually sink into oblivion and despair. Breathing its thick heavy air reduces the traveler's spirit to a state of total lethargy, causing it to collapse in feeble exhaustion. Death finally embraces such souls, yet she can offer no consolation, for even she must hand over each soul to the grand spirit of Life, whence it was born. After a temporary repose and counsel with the Great Ones, all souls return to the Earth for further purification.

The soul journey can be delayed, but never avoided. The only escape from pain and sorrow is to awaken from lethargy and to move forward. All who call out to Hope will be guided by her. She will lead them past mediocrity's rocky hills and gloomy valleys to the roads of struggle and yearning.

The path of yearning is fraught with falling boulders and stones which pierce and sting the heart, and falling trees and branches that tear at the mind and emotions. Yet while on this road, the traveler is ever mindful of the journey's goal – the celestial fields of paradise whose sight is vaguely beheld in dreams.

Falling obstacles on this road can never completely block their vision because Hope transmits guidance from their own heart via wind currents of love. Yearning's painful stings only enhance the desire to complete the soul journey. Doubt, despair, and sadness can fling their arrows, but Love will diminish their pain. When the torrential storms of confusion and anger attempt to halt those crossing the bridge of struggle, the prayers of those who trust in something greater than themselves, release the rays of sunshine to swallow up ominous clouds. Fear can grip the traveler for a time, but Love will release its strongest clutch. One by one valiant souls complete the journey to the celestial fields. With each new arrival, Fear's power dwindles, and Hope's strength increases, allowing her to penetrate the inner depths of callous hearts so Love can dress their wounds and ease their pain.

The diminished suffering will renew their strength, and these souls will soon be healed enough to recommence their journey. During slumbers, they will dream of the celestial fields of paradise. Their faint memories upon awakening will attract them to the path of yearning and struggle. Armed with courage and faith, they will journey until they arrive home!

"There's no place like home," I whispered as I set the book on the table. "I need to read these writings when I am depressed." And to think, the words came so easily and effortlessly.

Chapter Five

Oh, My Soul

The next few days I was busy with practical things that needed tending to. I welcomed a little inactivity from my inner world, but the following Monday, my divine guest showed up bright and early. I was beginning to enjoy sleeping and dreaming in ways I never had before or even thought possible.

Mr. Divine was casually dressed in denim jeans and a bulky knit multi-colored sweater, and brand new white Nike walking shoes. I knew the chill in my kitchen would be ebbed away by the fireplace. When he looked at me, I melted into those deep, penetrating, mysterious, blue eyes. There was so much I wanted to ask him, so much I wanted and needed to talk about, but the look in his eyes told me to be patient. Questions and queries could wait. Mr. Divine was my guest and it was my responsibility to make him comfortable. He waited for me to speak.

"Would you like to sit over here by the fireplace? I will pull the coffee table close by and you can enjoy the warmth of the fire while I brew some coffee," I said excitedly.

"It is so comfortable and cozy in this kitchen."

"I spend a lot of time in this room. I even have a computer set up in the back corner where I do some writing. I like a warm fire in an otherwise cold room; it seems to take me to another place and time. Does that make sense to you?" I stammered the question to him.

"Right now I am more interested in that delightful robust scent that is drifting throughout this kitchen. I want to drink the aroma in," Mr. Divine soothingly spoke.

"It is flavored coffee, Hazelnut, one of my favorites that I thought you might enjoy. It never needs cream nor sugar; it bellows flavor before it is even tasted," I explained.

"Let's just sit and sip for awhile. I want to know that you hear with your heart," he said with his eyes lazily closed, his hands wrapped around the hot coffee cup that was resting on his lap.

I could actually hear the silence. How do I explain this? I know it sounded strange, but I just knew I could hear the silence. What was the silence saying? What was the explanation of the sounds? I took another sip and slipped into another place, along side Mr. Divine. Where were we going? my mind kept asking and the silence kept speaking. How long would it take before I could understand the language of the silence?

Moments passed. Perhaps hours or even days. I had completely lost count of time. I was in another world far away from here. In this world, the silence ruled. After what seemed an eternity, I began to hear from the gentle wells of the silence a soft murmur. I leaned and cocked my head forward and Mr. Divine gently spoke these words.

"Michael, the Silence is a good mentor and friend. It bestows many gifts for those who take the time to listen."

"I have received many writings after being in the silence. There were times when I would spend two or even three hours in silent meditation. I noticed that my writings became deeper, and I think much better and clearer after some of those long meditations. And to think some people consider meditation a waste of time. One of my favorite 'writings,' *Oh my soul,* came to me after a long meditation. It confirmed my belief and need for time in the silence and solitude."

Mr. Divine's eyes lit up in a twinkling glow. "I would love to hear *Oh my soul*, Michael."

"It is a writing that I have memorized."

"I know," he said smiling.

I closed my eyes and with much honor and excitement, I slowly recited *Oh my soul* to my most supreme guest.

Oh, my Soul!

Oh, my Soul!

I hardly knew you at all.

Wasted years I spent chasing happiness and peace through ephemeral satisfactions only to have them disappear being replaced by the illusory goblins of bitterness, yearning, and sorrow. I have been an actor hiding behind the mask of delusion. How could anyone possibly know me when I have been disguised from myself? After so many performances of counterfeit roles, I began disappearing into the facade, gradually losing all sense of self.

Oh, my Soul!

Why did I lock you away in the somber dungeon of forgetfulness where the dark shadows and cobwebs of pain and suffering nearly blurred your image beyond recognition? Is it no wonder there was only deadness and hollow emptiness inside my heart? I ignored your cries until they dwindled to mere faint whispers I heard only in moments of quiet desperation, whose only power was to evoke a black incomprehensible sadness which disappeared with the night only to return again and again to haunt me.

Oh, my Soul, such estrangement and alienation from you embittered my heart, suffocating my life way with the ropes of apathy and despair. How I feared those vague moments of reverie when my heart heard your solemn faint echoes.

Oh, my Soul! How have you survived such abandon? How you kept from being mercilessly devoured by my doubts and fears is a mystery I cannot penetrate. Perhaps you fled during my nights of restless sleep, receiving nourishment and inspiration from some unknown source beyond mortal confines. Perhaps there you drank from magical rivers to renew your strength.

The source of your life is an enigma to me, but need I know your origin nor understand you to love you, beseech you for help, and in humble gratitude accept your gifts? My intuition says no. Despite my fear of becoming a walking incarnation of death, I cried out to you to rescue me from the lonely pit of despair and agonizing solitude. Utterly exhausted, I hobbled to the mirror hoping you would show me your face. Slowly, I opened my eyes and beheld a radiant smile I had not seen before.

"Oh, my Soul," I cried in tearful ecstasy. "You still live."

"Yes," an inner voice replied, "and so will you. Your call was the key to release me from the dungeon of forgetfulness and death. Henceforth, you will be embraced by life."

"Oh, my Soul, your strength is slowly bringing life back to me, awakening and resurrecting buried hopes and dreams. Like a child, I am comforted by your embrace. In your heart dwells the secrets and answers to life which you are imparting to me."

"I will lock you away no more. I open my mind and heart to you. My nightmarish slumber is over. It is time to merge in your love and then share my story with others who would hear the voice of their soul.

"Oh, my Soul, at last, my heart to thee do I wed!"

I softly repeated the last line over and over, "Oh, my Soul, at last, my heart to thee do I wed!" I opened my eyes slowly. It felt like I was floating in the air. I don't think I had ever felt so calm and serene. Mr. Divine seemed to glow even more than usual. His eyes were closed and I sensed that he was in another place. I wanted to ask him what he thought of *Oh my soul,* but the mere thought of talking seemed inappropriate and even cumbersome. I closed my eyes again. Perhaps I could somehow go to that magical place of mystique where he was. Perhaps the silence could take me there?

Chapter Six

On Love

It was February 14th when we had our next visit. It was 6 a.m. and I had had a restless night, drifting in and out of sleep. My mind was going a mile a minute. Finally, my rambling thoughts subsided and I fell back asleep. Moments later Mr. Divine approached me with the biggest smile on his face. He was wearing pink sweat pants and a white sweat shirt with a big red heart on it.

"Wow," I exclaimed. Then I realized it was Valentine's day. "How time surely does fly and perhaps more so when Cupid is in charge. Just what is this love thing all about?"

"It is about everything wonderful and special that makes the world go round," Mr. Divine said, motioning me to join him at the table.

"Good morning. So have you come to wish me a Happy Valentine's Day?"

"As a matter of fact, I have. I want to remind you that love is the most wonderful thing in the whole wide world. It forms the cord and energy that binds and unites form and matter; it connects you to everyone and everything that has ever been, is, or ever shall come into existence in any shape or form."

"Since love is the most wonderful thing there is, is it also a feeling?"

"Of course it is. Feelings are very real and live in your heart. But as Cupid exemplifies, love is multi-faceted and has many forms. It possesses many faces – physical, spiritual and mental. It truly is all there is on a certain level and all that you need. When love saturates you, everything you could possibly need or wish for manifests automatically for as I said, love is all there is."

"That reminds me of a Beatles song – 'All you need is love.'"

"Well put. Some of the greatest truths are revealed in songs. Since love is such a popular topic that is written about, sung about, hoped for, yearned for, putting people in all kinds of predicaments and circumstances, some joyous, some sorrowful, many a combination of both. Now let us talk more about love.

"Cupid comes from distant upper realms and lands upon human shores so that he might show off his cupidic (my new word for the day) beauty and magnificent form. He also comes to pierce the human heart with his arrow all for the purpose of reminding mortals that love both interacts with and transcends mortality. It is both immortal and mortal just as Cupid is. Being the son of beautiful Venus, he is capable of doing quite a number on mortals just as his mother is."

"I thought that Venus and the gods and goddesses were only myths and legends. They are not real."

"Says who?"

"Says, if I recall correctly, my professors in college who said the gods and goddesses are mythical creations as a tool for instructing and educating."

"Well, they are wrong, and maybe you should sign up for a new course. But we are not going to get into a deep metaphysical discussion of gods and goddesses at this time. Suffice it to say, they are as real as the air you breathe, although you may not be able to see them. Some people do see and believe in them. As a matter of fact, you've had a few visions of them yourself."

"That is probably just my over active imagination after watching *Zena the Warrior Princess* episodes or operas and movies."

"Well, at least you are open-minded enough to say probably. But we are not getting into a deep philosophical talk now."

"Is there really a course on such things?"

"Of course."

"Nice Pun."

"Thank you and speaking of courses, let me say that you know far more than you give yourself credit for. You have even contributed to the grand cosmic course on love through several of your writings. They are regarded and highly loved and appreciated on many dimensions. You are far more popular than you give yourself credit for."

"I always thought not many folks care about what I have to say."

"I care and several magazines have cared and more people are going to care as you let your writing flourish once more and your muse speak. Speaking of which – you demonstrated many years ago that you have a profound understanding of 'just what this love thing is all about' as you refer to it. You speak of soul love in several of your writings."

"I doubt anybody wants to read such far out stuff."

"You might be surprised. And what is so bad about being far out?"

"I guess I was being symbolic."

"Good. Symbolism is a grand means to bring you closer to your true self."

"Yeah, maybe I ought to get the cymbals out and make some noise."

"That might not be a bad idea. Maybe we should summon Archangel Michael to sound his trumpet with power and gusto. Something has got to be done. It is time that love stopped getting a bad rap and be really understood for what it truly is. It is time for everyone to begin walking the sacred path that leads them to the sanctuary of love. Journey forth despite your doubts and fears and you will prove yourself worthy to enter love's sacred sanctuary."

"Hey, I recognize that last sentence. It's from my 'writing' *On Love.*"

"Michael, you act like you don't understand love, but you understand far more than you give yourself credit for. That writing and others prove it."

"It's different when I write. It's like I step into another world."

"You enter the world of your soul and your true self. I think that is a beautiful thing to do and if more people did it, the world would be a much happier place."

"I guess I do step into the realm of my soul when I write."

"Yes, and it is time for your ego to surrender to the embrace of your soul."

"Surrender to the embrace of your soul. Why, you are a poet, Mr. Divine."

"It takes one to know one."

"You are too kind."

"I am not too kind. One can never be too kind. Let me put it a different and perhaps better way. How about I love you because you are one of *my* kind; and also you are one of *a* kind, as is everyone. Michael, I love you as I love everyone. I am interested in you and your writing as I am interested in everyone. Part of the reason for these visits and the book that you will write, is to get across and remind people how much I do care about them. I very much want to be a part of their lives. I am not some distant patriarchal being with long white hair and beard dwelling high in the clouds in some palatial mansion with harps being played by cherubs. I do not spend my time watching angels flying about and spreading their wings. I do not stroll about on streets of gold when I am not administering this or that punishment for this or that sin which humans have committed. They got me all wrong. I am alive and well and express myself in many forms, human being only one. I have infinite love, compassion, and creative resources that know no limits, as do you. People need to be reminded of this, yet again."

I looked away, slightly embarrassed. "I believe what you are saying. It's just kind of challenging and difficult to change our beliefs when they have been around for so long and so many people are so narrow minded and have limiting beliefs about you. This talk seems kind of revolutionary."

"Perhaps it is and rightly so."

"I think of another Beatles song, "We need a revolution."

"You do and writing has always been one great means to awaken the sleeping masses."

"I think of Harriet Beecher Stowe's anti-slavery novel, *Uncle Tom's, Cabin, Life among the lowly*. It made such a powerful impact on American attitudes toward African Americans and slavery in the United States. The novel intensified the conflict that led to the American civil war. I know about the impact writing and books can have. I have to admit I'm just not used to having anyone so interested in my writing. Dad used to call me a book worm and made fun of me for loving to read and write. He also called me a sissy and some other names I don't wish to repeat."

"That is most unfortunate and wounded your tender heart deeply. I am here to befriend you and show you that I love and believe in you. I value what you have to say. Never forget this. Well, I shall take my leave now. You will recall this visit as usual and don't forget to read *On Love*. We will talk about it next time."

"Okay. I will go dig it out."

I woke up a few minutes later and immediately picked up *Soul Murmurs* and turned the page. *On Love* was the first one. I wrote it in 1991 in a French literature class a few days after I decided to leave the Ph.D. program to pursue my writing dream. While the professor was lecturing, I entered a dreamy state of mind and could hear words popping in my mind. I stopped taking notes in French and wrote *On Love*.

On Love

This word is as misunderstood by people as is the purpose for life itself. People chase after Love incessantly as though it were a commodity one could possess. The moment you think you have grasped Love, she evades you, leaving your soul filled with emptiness and longing. Like the wind, Love cannot be seen nor possessed. To understand her, you must penetrate the innermost depths of the heart then be willing to patiently wait for her to reveal herself.

You must prove yourself worthy and purify your thoughts and actions before Love will unmask herself. Love only appears to the meek and humble childlike souls who have tamed the selfish ego, relinquishing all desire to exploit and control. To seek happiness externally is to be unfaithful to your own heart, preventing the alchemical union of spirit and soul which must occur before Love appears to you.

Love is complete unto herself, remaining invisible to all who refuse to see themselves for whom they truly are; whole and complete souls. Empty hollow hearts will never see Love through the eyes of another until they first see her through their own. How many people attempt to understand this simple truth? Very few, therefore frustrated and lonely, they fall in the arms of illusion's embrace, hoping this or that person will fulfill their deep longing for love, giving them a sense of wholeness.

They do not understand that the soul is complete and whole unto itself because it is part and parcel of love. No person can offer wholeness to another. People no longer remember who they are. They have by their own free will separated themselves from the deepest part of their essence – love.

If you would be soothed by Love's delicate caresses, go within, searching and searching until you find her. Call out to Love. She will whisper and direct you towards her. Journey forward despite your doubts and fears and you will prove yourself worthy to enter Love's sacred sanctuary. Persistent, diligent steps will lead you to the golden portal through which you will pass, arriving at Love's sacred wedding altar where she awaits you. Her kiss will awaken you from mortal oblivion, then you will never again feel lonely or incomplete.

There at the sacred altar your ego and soul will be wed. Then you will no longer search outside yourself for completion. It is at this time, and this time only, that Love can make herself visible to you through someone else's eyes. In reality, your Beloved's gaze will mirror your own image, and your gaze will mirror their reflection. For then you will realize that Love, Beloved, and Lover are one!

I sat still for a long time. I just could not move. The words kept ringing in my ears. A few minutes later I went to the kitchen and poured myself a soft drink. When I came back, I reread *On Love*. It was hard to believe that I wrote it. I sat back in my chair and soon fell asleep. Mr. Divine spoke to me immediately. "So now are you convinced that you know more about love than you give yourself credit for?"

"I guess maybe some part of me does."

"No maybes here and that someone is the voice of your soul. In the writing, you simply spoke a truth that every soul knows: that you cannot experience the wholeness and the fullness of love outside yourself with anyone until you experience it internally first. Then Love simply mirrors herself from everyone else around you. People's false perceptions and their fears are what keep them from knowing Love in its fullness."

"From my experiences with human love I must be on the bottom of the totem pole."

"Far from the bottom. Love is going to become a completely different experience for you, and rereading your writings is going to help you to get there. I hope you no longer doubt that you are in communion with the divine, whose very essence is this deep soul love we are talking about; it is your true essence too."

"I am beginning to think there might be something to it."

"Some thing. How about every thing to it. *On Love* was inspired from the very depths of your soul. Poetry is a very potent and expressive language of the soul. Embrace your poetic self, and fall in love with it and watch Love completely transform your life."

"Am I really ready for that?

"What do you think?"

"I am afraid to think."

"There is no rush. You can come back to this later. Remember, this is Valentine's Day. Now, I must take my leave. Let Love fill your entire being on this special day and remember that romantic love or Eros is but one face or facet of love" Mr. Divine said. Then, giving me a cavalier bow, he disappeared.

Chapter Seven

The Language of Love

"Valentine's day," I said when I woke up. "Yes, this is Valentine's day." For some reason my "writing" *The Language of Love* was strongly on my mind. Maybe I was just making it all up to give myself a reason and motivation to dig out my old writings. Well, what is the harm in that? They are inspirational writings and maybe there is some wisdom from them I can gain. With that thought in mind, I started thinking back to the time I wrote *The Language of Love.*

I remember the day I wrote it very well. I had awakened from troubled dreams. Somehow, I could not escape the gnawing tugs and pulls. I did not feel that I was who I thought I was. I kept touching my arm, looking in the mirror, and asking who the real me was. It even felt strange to be speaking English. All morning I could not shake this uneasy feeling that something very important was missing – that some very special component of my identity was missing. Then I heard a whisper in my mind, "Your 'forgetful self' veils who you really are. It is time to see past the veil." After lunch at the jewelry shop where I was working, I took pen and paper out and wrote:

The Language of Love

I look at people walking down the street and think, *You are not who you think you are. This is all a dream. It is not real.* Then I look at me and say, "You are not real, either." What is real? I need to know. I need to see. I need to feel what is real. I want to communicate by some means other than human language, something that connects me to all life, not separates me from it.

Perhaps I want to enter the realm of the "nameless," or rather, experience myself in all things and people. I try so hard to express my soul in human form and through human words. How can the realm of the soul be conveyed through human words? I feel very strongly that there were times when communication was much deeper and far more complete than it is now. I believe that words can barely touch the essence of another being. Yet, I have not found out what can.

Why do I feel so alienated from everything and everybody? I hear a voice in my head laughing and saying, "You are alienated because you are pretending that everyone and everything are other than you. Wake up! This perception is not real. The feelings, the alienation, the illusions, the separation, you and All That Is are one."

"Oh," I respond, "why does my ego keep forgetting?"

"Because another name for your ego is your 'forgetful self'."

"So, if we are all part of each other, then maybe people make me uncomfortable because they remind me of my 'forgetful self'. Is it possible for me to look at them and be spared some forgetfulness? Can I shut out some of the noises and distractions so as to commune with my real self?"

"Yes," the voice responded. "Who do you think I am? I am your soul, or your 'real self'."

"Oh," I exclaim, "I think I felt you around when I listened to some Buddhist chanting earlier. The internal dialogue shut off for awhile."

I try to keep my attention focused on my "real self". I do not look out the window at the shop where I am working. I do not see the people pass. I do not try to imagine what they are feeling or thinking. Is it possible that they are also in touch with their "real selves" right now? If they are me, and I them, then how can we be any different? I wondered.

When someone comes in the stores, or the phone rings, I find myself jumping into the role of the "not self," or the "forgetful self," and simply say nothing or make an effort to speak the language of the "real self," whatever that is. Would they understand me? Why wouldn't they if they and I are one?

The customers look at incense, buy nothing, and we exchange goodbyes as they leave. Oh, sweet relief! The "forgetful me" walks out of the door. I put on some opera and lose myself in the music for awhile. Leontyne Price is singing from the opera *Madama Butterfly*. I hear no words, only music, even though she is singing words in Italian. The music is transcendent. I am closer to the source. I am in communion with my "real self." Nothing outside is real except as it is a reflection of my internal world. I am not affected by my "forgetful self/selves" outside. The music is a bridge between me and them. It gives me comfort.

Then I hear the voice again, "Remember, there is no me and them; there is only the 'great I' playing diverse forms."

"Playing," I repeat, and smile with glee like a child.

I put on a tape of piano music in the stereo. This music is even more transcendent than the opera. There are no voices, no words, just pure sweet piano music. I close my eyes and absorb the notes one by one, allowing them to caress and soothe the very cells of my body. It is as though the music takes me to the realm of silence, to the realm where understanding and wisdom are communicated via non-sensory means and speak different languages which human words and sounds cannot even approximate.

Soon a man, his wife, and his child enter the store. "How are you?" he asks. I smile and say hello.

"You," I repeat to myself, "Oh no, my 'forgetful self' has returned. It thinks in terms of 'you' instead of 'I' in my diverse forms and beings. The little boy, who looks to be around five, says something to his mother. I want to put my hands over my ears and block out his words because they seem so foreign to me, even though he is speaking English.

I walk towards the stereo and turn up the piano music, thinking that it will drown out their talk. The little boy looks at me and smiles. Our eyes lock. No words are spoken. Suddenly, I realize that our 'I's are in communion. His gaze leads me past the noise to the silence and the real. I see him. I see me. We are one!

There is no need for music now. The mother motions for the boy to follow them out. "Bye," the boy says to me, waving.

"Goodbye," I respond, feeling warmth and love permeate my entire being. Suddenly, I see past the illusions, past the non-real. I see me for who I really am. I realize that love is the only essence there is. All else is illusion.

I feel peaceful the rest of the day. I do not hear words, voices, or music. I am grateful to the child for reminding me that the only true language is the language of love!

The words, the only true language is the language of love kept ringing in my ears. "Boy, no wonder everyone is hung up on this love thing," I said, out loud. "There is just so much more to it than we can imagine. Human Love. Divine Love. Maybe one day I would understand it all, or better still become it. I said the word "love" a few times and the sounds went all through me, caressing my every cell and atom. The sound was soft, and very pleasing. Then warmth filled me. It felt like every cell in my body was being bathed and embraced by a gentle sense of peace and love. I was in the mood to do something very spontaneous. I kept thinking back to February 14th of 1988 when I wrote *All That Is.*

I am a part of all that is.
All That has been and all to be born.
When the spark of life takes me from this Earth,
I shall be greeted by the new morn.

Feeling full of love I knew I had to express it. Mr. Divine had told me to let love fill my entire being and that romantic love was but one face or facet of love. So I quickly got dressed and off I went. I went to the store and bought a bunch of candy. Then I went out and played Cupid for a couple of hours. I met five older women sitting on park and bus benches. I struck up brief conversations and told them that they were beautiful and sweet and they must never forget it.

Poetic verses popped in my head so I shared them. I even sang them a love song, then handed them some candy. Only one lady seemed remotely suspicious, but she warmed up after we talked awhile. Some would consider me a nut case, but I did not care. I felt love moving in and through me. I had to move the energy and pass it on. Let people think what they would. Mr. Divine had reminded me of some things I had felt and written about many years ago. It was time to embrace my soul and the soul of others. It was time to embrace "the real self" expressing through me and others. A holiday such as Valentine's Day especially gives us that very opportunity. It gave me great joy to tell those women that they were sweet hearts. I told a friend many years ago that if I let my guard down, I would fall in love with every body. It was wonderful that this day I had let that guard down and brought some sunshine and sweetness into the lives of some fellow humans.

I was still on a roll. When I got back home, I picked up the phone and called everyone I knew to wish them a Happy Valentine's Day. I even dialed a few wrong numbers purposefully and wished a few strangers the same thing. One lady hung up on me, but two others thanked me. I watched a movie then went to bed and slept better than I had in weeks.

Chapter Eight

I am Life

I awoke before sunrise half expecting the Valentine cheer to disappear along with the breaking of a new day. I found that I was still thinking about love. But what to do on February 15th? I did not have the nerve to go out again and be the jolly minstrel. *Maybe I'd write something new today*, I thought, yawning. *But not right now.* I turned over and fell back asleep.

Moments later Mr. Divine appeared and I heard that special voice I have come to recognize, "Why can't everyone be your sweet heart? Why can't love go on infinitely?" Why can't that feeling go on eternally? Today and each day and in every way. Each day can still be Valentine's Day. Love can be expressed in so many ways; sexual expression being only one small minute aspect of its vastness. This is why you can fall in love with everyone. It is time you experienced more love."

"Good morning Mr. Divine. I thought you were going to get philosophical on me and tell me that I need 'to become love' since you recently said that love is all there is."

"Well, actually being and experiencing are two sides of the same coin, Michael. On the relative worlds, it is possible to both 'be' and 'experience' love."

"So am I supposed to go out today and tell everyone how special they are?"

"That would be great. Yesterday you were in a spontaneous mood and you followed your bliss and spread some love. You really ought to do it more often. You have Christmas everyday. Why not Valentine's Day?"

"I have Christmas alone in the privacy of my home. There, no one can call the men in white coats."

"I guess you have done enough for awhile. Didn't it feel good to make those women smile? Like I said before, love is simply the greatest thing there is. Your writing, *I am Life,* reiterates that and quite nicely I must add. There are several synonyms for me. A couple of those synonyms are life and love. You all are familiar with the phrase, God is Love. But how many of you have ventured to say I am Love, or better yet, I am God, or even better yet, *I am Life?* I explained how I know myself through my creations; the way I come into the fullness of my being is to know myself experientially. Your little writing was one way for me to know and glimpse myself in my experientialness, my new word for the day."

"So, are you saying that I did not write it, but you did?"

"Yes and no. You are part of me and I part of you, or even more accurately, you are me and I am you. So yes, I wrote *I am Life,* and yes you wrote it, too. In a way, we wrote it to ourselves and to each other. The issue for you was that it was such a potent expression of creativity that you thought you were going too far. You had a hard time imagining yourself as being all the elements that the writing talks about. Fire. Wind. Water. Earth. I find this amusing since you have stated that you are a part of all that is in other writings."

"Well, stating and actually experiencing are two different things."

"Stating it is important. Experiencing is even more so. The truths that you reveal and revere are not fully internalized until they are experienced. I want you to read *I am Life* and instead of seeing just yourself writing and making this fabulous declaration, see 'me' talking to myself. This way the writing will make more sense."

"I hope so. I'm beginning to think maybe you are going to wind up in the loony bin along side me."

"That might be interesting. Well, I need to take my leave now so you can locate *I am Life.* Try to give a little Intro like you do for the others. We'll talk about it at our next visit."

The next thing I knew I was awake and looking for the writing. Before reading it, I recalled Mr. Divine asking me to give some background. I racked my brains to see what was going on back then. Oh yes, how could I ever forget? That was written during a very difficult time. I was meditating a lot and having some profound spiritual experiences. I went on a lot of what I call mythic journeys. Various characters and heroes from my inner world were paying me visits and taking me on all kinds of journeys. My dream life was very active. This was rewarding because I was feeling the pangs of human loneliness. I seemed to experience nothing but disappointments when it came to relationships. I just was not able to find the right person to connect with on the level I yearned to connect. I cannot even explain or define this connection. I just know that it involves something beyond human interactions; some adventures and journeys into the domains of the soul. I wanted to lose myself in the presence of someone such as I have done twice in my life.

To look deeply into my old love's eyes somehow took me outside of myself. I was pulled in and drawn into another world. That is the only way I know how to explain it. I could never look at her for long because I feared where her gaze would take me, although I longed for that very thing. Something similar happened with another friend. I would actually get dizzy and it seemed that the floor beneath my feet was dropping a few inches when I looked into his eyes. I could look at chairs and even see their atomic structures in their moving forms and patterns. As crazy as that sounded, that is exactly what I was thinking and feeling.

During this time I managed to keep body and soul together via various jobs. I did some Psychic Readings. I did some singing telegrams and some tutoring of languages for extra money. I house sat for several people for room and board. I wrote a lot. I sent things out. A few poems, stories and articles got published. Nothing big, but big enough bites to make me want more. I dreamt. I hoped. I yearned. One day I remember thinking I just can't take this anymore. Life on the Earth is unbearable. I can't go on being estranged from my own soul and spirit. I had addressed that estrangement and alienation in *Oh, my Soul*. I just couldn't seem to be able to experience in daily human life the feelings of joy and love that embraced me in my meditations, reveries and dreams. I wondered why I was even on the Earth as I know many people have asked that question during dark times.

A few days later, I woke up at four a.m. feeling the heaviness of my body. I had been having some powerful flying dreams. My spirit wanted to soar. "What does it all mean?" I pleaded. The questions continued in my mind.

Finally, in my despair, I lay still and cried. A time later I began to drift off. Instead of soaring like I usually did, this time I was descending, falling, going somewhere very dark and deep. It felt like I was falling into the void. The abyss. The bottomless pit. Strangely enough, I was not as enveloped with fear as before. I finally managed to open my eyes and I saw a little ray of light slightly above my head. It glimmered and glowed and looked like a tiny star. A small glimmer of hope I remember thinking. As I kept descending, I heard the words "Higher, Higher, Higher. Then "Deeper, Deeper, Deeper. I am falling deeper in love with humanity. I am taking in their sorrows, their joys, their unknowing and their hopes. Then I woke up. I took out my pen and paper. It took a few minutes to come back to myself enough to think coherently let alone write. But a few moments later, the words just poured effortlessly.

I am Life

Higher. Higher. Higher. Deeper. Deeper. Deeper. More and more each day. I am falling in love with humanity. They are growing inside me. I am expanding to contain them. Joyous stretching of my being. I touch their minds, their hearts, their dreams. Their smiles are becoming my smiles. Their heartaches and joys the makers of my tears. Shreds of clinging fade away. Diaphanous mists that conceal me are melting and disappearing.

The selfish me is stepping aside. Moving through life. Soaring above. Swimming in the waters of love, playfully. Jumping about. Flying higher and higher. Plunging deeper. Glimpsing the heavy land and souls. The lost forgotten ones need to be remembered. I want to touch them, give part of me to them so they can become whole.

I am radiant, golden fire sparks. Dancing. Singing. Shining. Touching all life and changing it. Burning away hurt and sorrow. I am wind, blasting and strong. Breath of life I give them. Let me suck in their unknowing and despair. I am the gentle zephyr, calm, caressing and stroking their face with my coolness. I make them smile and reach out to life. Open their mouths, yawn, relax. Take in life. More and more. I am waters rapid, and still.

I am bubbling, placid brooks. I am crashing roaring waves beating fiercely against the shore. I fill them with tingly wetness, exciting and stimulating them with abundant pleasure. Always room for more. Take in your fill then save some for tomorrow, or better, come back and sup with me. Let us enjoy each other.

I am earth, hard, muddy, leafy green. Torrential storms. Trees dancing in ecstatic frenzy as I uproot them from their attachments. I am crops growing, extending my grasp towards the sun. Digging my roots deep into the earth. I am blue sky. I am the dawn and the sunset. The dancing fluffy clouds. Let me touch you. Atoms dance and mate. I am the maker of music. I am giving birth to more of you, and me. More of you to taste, touch, see, smell and hear life's delights sensual and sweet.

I am Life hungry for itself. Needing itself. Yearning for itself. Life crying for itself as a mother cries for her lost babe. Clinging to you as the tree root clings deep and hard into the earth. As I know you more, I become more of myself. As you know me, you become more of yourself. Not fragmenting, splitting, and fading into meaningless nothingness. But oneness. Wholeness.

I am Life! Giver and Sharer of Dreams. Won't you reach out to me. Embrace me. Press me close to your heart. Let me stir and awaken the fires inside you. Won't you love me?

Whoa, is that some heavy stuff. I knew this was not a writing for thinking; it was one to experience and lose myself in. To lose myself in the words to the point that I actually transcend them and experience their essence. That made me wonder if I was losing it. I read it again and felt so strange that I had to put it away and shove away the thoughts that were gushing into my mind. I spent the next few days doing everything I could *not* to think about it and what all it might imply. Slowly, my curiosity started nagging at me and I began to wonder what Mr. Divine would have to say about *I am Life*. The next morning he showed up promptly and he had a lot to say.

"So you think you were losing your sanity. You were losing something, alright, but it was not your sanity. It was your insanity. Your spirit was taking your ego for a ride, expanding your consciousness and your awareness. When your ego glides on the wings of the soul for a ride, you see so many more vistas few humans imagine possible. As you say, "Flying higher and higher." As exhilarating as this is, it can still be frightening and unsettling while you are in the midst of the experience. You cannot sort it out during that time. And there really are countless places the spirit can visit via soul flight. When you soar, you also plunge. Learn from nature. Behold an eagle or falcon and watch it soar and stretch its beautiful wings so wide you would think it could encompass an entire world. Then watch it dive and plunge. To soar and to plunge or to take flight and enter the depths take you to the center of your being and to the center of life itself. They are just two different ways to get there. The writing is about sacred soul movement which is called stepping or merging into the sea of your greater being. This is, by the way, one of the reasons you have many water and flying dreams. It is a way of soaring and delving into the seas of your greater being – the dream being a symbolic reenactment of such experiences."

"I do see water a lot when I have flying dreams. I soar and plunge, but I never land in the water. I come close, but never fall into the water. And there was water this time, too. As fascinating as this all was I have to confess that part of me thought that the writing sounded like some drug-induced hallucination."

"Tell me how it made you feel, Michael."

"I found that my thoughts were racing. My heart told me to stop analyzing the experience and just write down the thoughts that came to me. So I continued."

"Now, just as your spirit was taking your ego for a ride and a journey into the sea of your greater being, I, on the other hand, was making a grand plunge and stepping into the sea of my lesser being. I was falling and constricting my being so that I could experience humanity. You were stretching your being to experience part of your greater 'Isness' and connection with me. We were doing the same thing in different ways. Our souls were being pulled and stretched so that we could contain the other. Your spirit wanted to soar. You were reaching upward for me. I wanted to descend from the realm of the absolute and visit my relatives to insert a pun. I wanted to partake of my relative nature which is also part of my material nature. You were going up. I was going down. Then we shifted and traded places.

"If you will recall, the first three words you heard were Higher. Higher. Higher. Then you heard the words: Deeper. Deeper. Deeper. You were reaching upward while I was reaching downward. In reality, you were trying so hard to get to me and I was reaching down for you. You were not consciously aware of me communicating and this is why the writing made you feel strange. There were a lot of energies being exchanged in this writing, call them strange if you will, but only in the sense that they were different. The first part, "Deeper. Deeper. Deeper and more each day I'm falling in love with humanity," is you speaking.

"I am expanding to contain them – and I add that it is a joyous stretching of my being – that is me speaking. Ask a mother how it feels when her baby moves inside her womb. It may unsettle her, at least the first time or so, but she also feels awe and wonder. In a sense I, or the universe, which is part of me, is like one big gigantic mother who is constantly getting knocked up, to insert some humor. Except that I am impregnating myself with my creations; humanity being merely one of them. Not only do I create life and each of my children, but I create the elements as well and partake of their splendors. I am radiant, golden fire sparks. Touching all life and changing it and burning away hurt and sorrow. I can do that for you, you know – burn away your hurt and sorrow. Tell me, overall, how did the experience make you feel?"

"It was exhilarating in a strange way. It seemed so real. I felt like the wind, the fire, and the earth. I know it sounds so weird and hokey, like I was definitely smoking some good weed."

"You don't need to smoke weed because you are naturally high on life. Now isn't that an interesting phrase. High on life. When you are high on life, you are in contact with your soul, you are soaring, and it feels natural. To be high is natural. Some of the flower children of the 60s knew more than they got credit for. So tell me, do you really think this writing sounds like a drug-induced hallucination?"

"At first, I thought I was hallucinating, but that didn't last long because I don't do drugs. I was dreamy and yearny, my new word. I really like some of the phrases in the writing. "Let me suck in their unknowing and despair." Boy, what I'd have given for years to get an offer like that. You know how I've struggled with despair all my life."

"I know."

"This writing is getting more exciting to me. It's like some part of me just memorized it. I love the idea of you touching our minds, our heart and our dreams. Our smiles becoming your smiles. That's very nice. Makes me get all feely good inside and tingly. You say our heartaches and sorrows are the makers of your tears. Well, that makes you seem downright human. Gee, maybe we really are never alone. Maybe there is a God up there, or inside us, or wherever, that really does care about us. Wow, I'm getting filled up with hope."

"Good. I do care about you and you are never alone. If I get nothing else across through this book or any other book; if I can help you to see that you are never alone, I will be a happy camper."

"You know this all somehow makes sense to me. I can't explain or express how. It's really far beyond words. Wonder if I'll wake up in the morning and think this is all nuts?"

"I don't think so. Once you've had an epiphany, you are forever changed."

"After listening to you, now I think, how could I not know that this little inspirational writing was you talking to yourself and to me as well as to others."

"Can you now accept that it is also you talking to yourself and others?"

"I think so and it makes me feel very good inside. I am seeing an image of me at the park a long time ago. I was lying on the ground taking deep breaths. I remember fearing that I was about to explode. Now it seems that maybe I was just expanding. They tell women during childbirth to take deep breaths and push, push, push. Maybe I was expanding and stretching on a symbolic level."

"Yes, you were pregnant in a metaphorical sense. You were giving birth to hopes, dreams and aspirations."

"That has always been such a struggle for me. No wonder, at times, I felt so crazy all I could do was to lie on the ground and just breathe hard. I guess the dreams got tired of being shoved down."

"You were making room for them, and to do that, you have to stretch your being and expand. This is what I am doing as I, we, express at the beginning of the writing. I do truly want you to take in your fill of life. Every time I communicate with you and you communicate with me, I am giving birth to more of you and me and vice versa. We are all in this together. You. Me. Everyone."

"This sounds like a science fiction movie. I can just see it now. The big Mr. Almighty, God himself giving birth and being a mother. Wonder what kind of reviews a movie like that would get?"

"Maybe some good ones if you write the script."

"Oh, I'm not up for that, at least not yet."

"Mr. Divine has infinite patience. I nurture every story line and idea you have stored away in that fine brain and subconscious mind of yours. You have written science fiction and fantasy before. You can do it again. I am very comfortable with those genres because you can get by with and do so much more with fiction."

"I am open to all possibilities."

"I am life hungry for itself.   Needing itself. Yearning for itself. As I know you more, I become more of myself. There is quite a bit of information in your little inspirational writings, Michael. They need to be shared."

"Thank you. I am life." I replied. "Giver and Sharer of Dreams. To think that God shares his dreams with us and wants to hear about ours is really beautiful." I closed my eyes. "Won't you reach out to me?" I whispered. "Embrace me. Press me close to your heart. Let me stir and awaken the fires inside you. Won't you love me? Dear God, what is happening to me? Am I losing my mind?"

"You are not losing your mind" Mr. Divine said softly, "You are finding it."   When I opened my eyes, he was no where to be seen.

Chapter Nine

I am

It was ten a.m. when I woke up and I'm usually up by seven. My head was lighter than a feather; it felt like I was still in the dream. I drank a big glass of water and took my vitamins. My eyes found their way to the painting of the long red-haired woman which hung on the kitchen wall. I always get lost in that painting; that woman seems so real. I sometimes even talk to her and joke about how I am going to one day step into that painting and take a stroll with her.

I walked around the house to get my bearings. After my recent experiences, I needed to get grounded. Not that my dream visits with Mr. Divine and my writing were not real, but I needed to experience a different kind of real – the feel of tangible objects. Yes, the house was solid matter with sturdy walls and hard floors. I rubbed the walls needing to touch things solid. I touched the cabinets, the table and chairs and other furniture. I picked up several objects and enjoyed feeling their texture. I took out some ice from the freezer and took in the coldness as I breathed into the glass. I closed my eyes and felt the lightness once more. It was as though part of me was floating. Was this how it felt to be a ghost? Part of me didn't seem to be here. Nothing seemed to be totally tangible. I didn't complain though. For the first time in days that little gnawing emptiness inside seemed to be gone. "Wow, I am not depressed," I exclaimed, then danced about, nearly slipping as I stepped on a sock that was lying in the middle of the floor. I walked around and touched more objects.

A few days later a friend invited me to visit her in Pittsburgh. Three days later I was on a Greyhound bus heading to one of my favorite cities. After two days in Pittsburgh, we went to Lily dale, New York to visit the famous spiritualist camp. It was a magical land come to life. Located in the New York snow belt, we were graced with light snow and a full-fledged snow storm the morning we left. We walked the hallowed grounds and took in the beauty of nature. We stayed at an old guest home. At night we played cards and shared laughs. What made a big impact on me was when Victoria shared two of her stories. It was obvious she loved these stories and thoroughly enjoyed telling them. Totally caught up in the story, I was eager to hear more when, to my surprise, she suddenly stopped.

"This is where I am blocked," she said in a pleading tone. "My character, Julian, is looking in a mirror, when suddenly he sees the image of someone behind him. Who is this person? What does he want? he wonders. Could it be a ghost? Is he having a vision? From that point I am stuck, Michael. I can't go any further."

Then the strangest thing happened to me – her character, Julian, started talking to me in my head. "I know where the story is going," I exclaimed. "Julian wants to kill himself. There is a razor and he wants to slash his wrists. There are several drops of blood in the sink, but it is not from the razor – it's from a nosebleed."

"Oh, my goodness," Victoria cried out, "that is wonderful, keep going."

For the next hour, I took the reigns and moved my friends' story forward. She took some notes to complete the scenes in full detail later. When I was finished, I was sweating and my heart palpitating. "I just didn't know what came over me."

"You were wonderful," Victoria praised. "Now, for the first time in years, I am going to be able to get past that block and finish my story. Thank you so much."

"I'm just glad to help," I replied, excited.

That experience affected me profoundly. It reminded me that my creative juices had not dried up. I had stepped into another world again – this time someone else's – and I was just as comfortable there as stepping into my own inner worlds. Time had once more stopped and the gnawing empty feelings and depression that haunt me so often abated as well.

I returned to my home two days later, still intrigued how I stepped into Victoria's story world so easily. I could see and describe her character as though he had been a true "in-the-flesh" person visiting us in the room. Such experiences were not totally unfamiliar to me. Although I had never talked to anyone else's character before, for years I had been talking to my characters, and vice-versa. Looking back, I realize that I sensed a long time ago that there is more to characters and stories than we are aware.

This was confirmed by something I read by Jane Roberts – paranormal, ESP, writer and channel of "the famous Seth Books." Most of her books were published as non-fiction, but she did publish her "Over Soul Seven" books as fiction. She explained in one of the books that "Over Soul" (the main character) began to talk in her head and give her advice. He would speak to her at odd times and not just when she sat down to write the novel. Over Soul played the roles of fiction character and mentor/spirit guide at the same time. Jane Roberts' experience with Over Soul Seven really got me to thinking because I had had some similar experiences which I had dismissed as fantasy.

After reading the book, I felt more comfortable with the idea that my story and novel characters have a life of their own, and can even visit us, though we be their so-called author. They can even play multiple roles. At this point, I began to entertain the possibility that perhaps the entire creative process of writing involves far more than we know about due to our limited knowledge on the subject. I began to take a different approach to my characters. I would chat with them and ask them questions when I needed advice. Some seemed content living within the realm of my imagination. Others were curious about my life and would visit me, and answer questions and give advice – which I might add – was very sound and helpful. This in itself made the experiences worthwhile; even if it all came from my unconscious mind. I wondered what Mr. Divine might have to say on the subject.

The next morning we shared a steaming mug of mocha cappuccino.

"Good morning, Michael. So you've been having some strange experiences! Characters from your stories talking to you in your mind and giving you advice? Whoa!"

"You probably think I have totally lost it."

"You have not lost it as you put it; on the contrary, you have found some very important knowledge. There is much more to story characters than most people are aware; they are far more than imaginary creations of the author. I will speak more on this later in a chapter you will title 'fantasy possesses elements of truth'."

"Thank you. I look forward to it and just hope I can wait that long – I'm so excited now."

"Now, let's talk about another literary character that you are fond of and who is fond of you – the poet, Walt Whitman."

"I think he is one of the best and most inspired poets of all times."

"I might also add that Mr. Divine is not the first to pay you a wee-hour morning visit. Walt Whitman paid you a visit some years ago and you dismissed the visit as an imaginary vision. You could relate to what he spoke about just as you relate to many of his poems. Walt could sense your thoughts and the impressions which your emotions emanated. Emotions extend themselves outward and generate spirals of energy which can move at lightning speeds through the ethers or atmosphere. The so-called 'dead' can sense those vibrations which are similar to transmitted radio waves. Walt projected an image of himself into your mind which you interpreted as something from your own imagination. On a certain level, he truly was there with you. When you told a friend about the experience your exact words were, "It seemed so real, but how can that be? My imagination must surely be working overtime."

"Let it suffice to say that *Morning Coffee with God* should not feel so bizarre considering some of the unusual experiences you have had."

"That makes sense, but why is it so hard to accept what my soul and heart tell me are true?"

"Because you live in a society that values what it can name, measure, define, label and logically explain. In your society, those are the things that are more accepted and approved of. It is not the same in some other civilizations. The realms of dreams, visions, mythology, fantasy, and clairvoyance are considered to be irrational, but among indigenous people throughout the world, such irrational experiences and events are accepted as common place. Your society does not especially favor 'the irrational' unless it comes from the domain of fiction and fantasy which it considers to be 'unreal'."

"Isn't it interesting how popular horror, sci-fi, fantasy and parnormal films are. Michael Myers just won't die in the 'Halloween' movies nor Jason in the 'Friday the 13th' movies. People flock back to the theatre for the latest installments."

"This shows that part of them does believe in 'the irrational' and has a need to experience it, albeit it vicariously through books, movies, and dreams."

"Part of me has never cared much what society thinks as long as I am a law abiding citizen and don't harm anyone."

"While another part of you has always been uncomfortable when you move into your 'greater being,' and when you step into different worlds. Don't you agree?"

"I live in a world of my own contradictions."

"Yes, you like most people do."

"Part of what has allowed me to continue living in this world is my ability to step beyond the third-dimension and visit other realms and worlds. I've always known they exist. Without the consolation and company of my imaginary friends and fantasy heroes and characters as a child, I think I would have gone crazy. Yet, when it comes to stepping into similar worlds as an adult, I sometimes fear I am losing it. It's enough to drive a lunatic even more bonkers."

"You have a good mind, Michael. I don't foresee the men in white coats coming for you. And not all of your inner friends are what you might call imaginary friends. Walt Whitman is certainly a real person and so are some others who have visited you before. Do you remember that evening Benjamin Franklin paid you a visit?"

"Yes I do. There was a big storm outside. I had lain down for a few minutes when his image suddenly appeared in my mind and I could hear him talking to me. It was so real."

"Ben Franklin paid you a mental visit."

"I remember thinking I must be making it all up. What I couldn't figure out was how real it all seemed. I could actually hear his thoughts as though he was talking in my head."

"That is what happens in a mental visit."

"Really? I also had the distinct impression that he took pleasure in paying me a visit, and perhaps shaking me up a bit."

"Isn't that the purpose of a storm?" to insert a little humor.

"I remember praying, 'Heaven, bless my soul, Benjamin Franklin has just paid me a visit.' Then I knew I was a candidate for the asylum."

"Heaven does bless your soul. Remember, the soul can be in many places at once; its perimeters are much broader and wider than most people imagine. Remember, if I am omnipresent then so can you be. If I can communicate with all life-forms and all people – which I can and often do – then so can you. Or better put, I am aware of this and most of you are not. Not being consciously aware of something does not invalidate it. As you open your minds and stretch your soul muscles, so to speak, so you will have more experiences and in time, they will cease to disturb you. Part of you does not accept or has not yet realized the vast potential of the soul. This is most unfortunate and accounts for the loneliness, alienation and fragmentation that so many people feel. You feel disconnected because you are. Your soul knows you are connected to all of life. You have always sensed it, but your ego finds it hard to accept experiences if they become too 'non-ordinary'. Then you wonder why you are depressed and lonely so often.

"During such times, you can find relief by stepping into the realms of fantasy. Fantasy is just a different version of reality or a reality existing on another plane and dimension. There are as many versions of reality as there are people. Ideas, emotions, thoughts and realities intermingle all the time. Not only can the soul be in more than one place at once, it can also glimpse its past and future selves in those places and realities. It can also view parallel worlds and realms completely different from life as you know it. The purpose of life is to create. I create. You create. We all create. There are infinite ways to create. You are learning how to simultaneously exist in more than one realm or dimension. In time, you will become more conscious that you are doing so.

"Each and every one of you are doing this at all times although most of this occurs at the subconscious and super-conscious levels. You are choosing to merge all your subconscious and super-conscious personalities into the one circle of consciousness they truly are. And when it's all sorted through and worked out for you, I have the hunch you are going to be one happy camper.

"You are going to know a 'love' and 'joy' few ever do. You have to remember that the love you seek is the love inside you. All these realms and other worlds are also within you. The masters are able to be in more than one world at a time. You are coming into mastery, Michael; you are being born anew. Jesus said, 'You must be born again before you can enter the kingdom of Heaven.' That is what we are talking about here. He also said, 'In my father's house are many mansions. If it were not so, I would have told you.' You are moving your consciousness and awareness into some of these other rooms.

"Some resort to drugs to maneuver their consciousness through different layers of their psyche. Others do so using meditation techniques or breathing exercises. There are many ways to alter perceptions as exemplified in shamanic teachings. Am I getting over your head now?"

"I can sort of follow what you are saying. Even though I sometimes fear I am losing it when I write, time stops. I step into different worlds and my soul is glad."

"You also lost yourself in other worlds when you used to take singing lessons and went on stage. Much more happened than you can begin to be aware of. Sometime we will go more into that."

"I really miss singing. A career as an opera singer would have been fulfilling."

"You are singing on another dimension. Now, it is time to hear another of your writings. Want to know which one comes to mind?"

"Sure."

"*I Am*. You know it by heart, don't you?"

"Yes."

"First, please tell your readers what was going on when you wrote it."

"Do I have to? That was such an awful time."

"I know."

"That period in my life was no piece of cake, to say the least. I had written quite a few stories and a few were published in small press magazines. I was a part-time substitute teacher and had my own singing telegram business. I felt that those I loved dangled carrots in front of me constantly. Now, I see that I was the biggest dangler of all. I would delve into this or that creative endeavor then pull away. I could have gone so much further with my singing telegram business.

"I was writing a lot during that time. I will never forget the critique I received from a famous writer. Handwritten on the bottom of my query letter was, "writing talent is inborn. Anyone can learn to plot. If I could do it, and I think I have very little talent, you certainly could." Needless to say, I was higher than a kite for weeks and still cherish that personal note from her. I worked very hard after that, learning how to plot better. I got a few more critiques, but no paying magazines bought my stories. I had two fantasy novels going as well. Finally, it just became too much. I could not get motivated to finish the novels. I concluded that I must be a mediocre writer.

"My frustrations got the best of me and I quit writing altogether. Several times, I cried myself to sleep, whimpering, "Why can't I get just a small break?"

"That night I had a dream. I was standing on a stage in a performing arts center in New York. It was some kind of gala charity performance and I had agreed to do a little dance routine.

I was dressed in a golden skin-tight body suit. On my forehead in bright, red, sparkling, letters were two words: I am. On my heart, where a big red heart was painted, was one word – art. The people clapped and waved their arms when I danced.

"Moments later I woke up softly repeating the words, 'I am art'. For the next few days, I felt strange and different. I was on the verge of losing myself in a sea of despair and hopelessness. I truly felt I was coming apart at the seams. I recall running in the park just to maintain some kind of grip on reality, and several times I had to literally grip and hold onto a tree to keep from slipping away. That night I prayed for deliverance. I told God that if something didn't change, I simply could not go on.

"I have learned that desperation often precedes the new dawn and heralds rebirth. A few days later, I awoke before daybreak after having terrible nightmares. I looked out the window and observed the glowing full moon. It was wrapped in a silvery mist and seemed to grow brighter and larger the more I looked at it. It even seemed to smile down upon me. I was slowly filled with an unexplainable feeling of serenity. 'It is time to write,' I heard in my mind, so I found pencil and paper and sat by the window and wrote *I am*. I liked it so much that I have memorized it."

"I'm all ears," Mr. Divine said and gave me his full attention.

I am

I awoke early before dawn feeling restless. When I calmed myself, a realization came bubbling to the forefront of my mind. It was something I had sensed a few times in my life but instantly pushed away. Too confronting. Too scary for me. What I came to know was this. There is no me! And yet I looked about and came to know more of myself.

I am the flight of the bird aiming for unknown destinies. I am the poet struggling to capture the wordless – the nameless. I am hunger and that which is consumed by the hungry. I am the song which fills the heart of the Lover. I am the Beloved which adores the voice of her Love. I am movement, dancing, swirling, spiraling in space, needing to touch infinity.

Needing to stretch my being and explore worlds small and

grand. I am the tears that spill from Sorrow's well, and the tears that pour forth when the heart is glad. I am the dreams which have been dreamt. Dreams being dreamt at this moment in time, and the dreams of tomorrow which nurture today. I am Love that cries and Love that sighs. Love that is born and Love that dies. Won't you touch me and let us be one!

"I am is my true name," Mr. Divine said with a big grin on his face. "If you will recall in the scriptures when Abraham asked me what my true name is, I told him – I am that I am. True words have been spoken very beautifully in your little writing; how amazing that your despair led you to such a fine creation. Despair is a powerful teacher and offers many gifts for those who face the dark nights of the soul. Your despair took you into the deeper world of your greater being.

"You stepped from 'the relative' into 'the absolute'. From duality into total oneness and back to duality. The writing spoke of your freedom and who you truly are – who I truly am-and who we collectively are. Children usually know this better than adults. Why do you think they lift their little arms pretending to be flying birds? Why do they imitate other animals, talk to trees, and to their imaginary friends? They know on a deep level that they are one with the birds, the other animals and the trees.

"Some of your highly sensitive artists also step into the 'sea of the great 'I am,' which is nothing less than the 'greater being' or 'self' that is the true essence of everyone. Since you have no paradigms which support and embrace these deeper concepts and knowledge, many are left to their own unfortunate devices for coping. When you doubt your ability to contact divinity directly, reread *I am*. Well, this has been a fine visit, but now I think you need to bask in the realm of 'the relative' for awhile."

What a profound conversation! I sat still for several minutes in total awe. A few minutes later I reached for paper and pen from my night stand and took notes. I was still amazed at how much I could recall. Was it possible to have photographic dream memory?

Over the next few days, I acquired a deeper appreciation of *I Am* and some other writings. Slowly, but surely, I was becoming convinced that God was communicating with me. I went to my book *Halfway to Heaven* and reread my writing *Message to my Soul* which I had written in May of 1984 while in the throes of unrequited love. I had ended the writing with the line, "I am with you always," but in the original version, I had ended it with "I am with you always. That Which Is."

I had goose bumps as I reread *I am*. Even then part of me sensed I was communicating with divinity although another part of me doubted. Now that God was talking to me directly in everyday common speech, albeit in dream visits, my beliefs were once more challenged. There just had to be more to these dreams than fantastical imaginary wanderings. The fact that I was having them so frequently said a lot as dream books and manuals advise us to pay special attention to repetitive dreams. The conversations were not the same, but the visitor was. Something profound and important was going on which I could not ignore. I also knew that I was not ready to share these dream experiences with anyone.

Yet my mind still had its doubts. It's one thing to read someone else's book who claims to communicate with God. Many people read the *Conversations with God* books by Neale Donald Walsch. Some of them like them; others are not impressed, and a few claim that the author made it all up. I could relate to all of the opinions, for at different times, I felt the same way and sometimes still do. It is quite bold to claim to receive messages from the Almighty. I wondered how many of the nut houses were filled with people who made similar claims. Weren't they labeled as schizophrenics? Then I thought of the joke "What is good about being schizophrenic? Schizophrenia beats dining alone." I always have a good laugh when I think about that joke.

The next morning my Divine visitor returned.

"How are you, Mr. Divine?" I asked.

"Fine and dandy, as usual. I like that little joke about schizophrenia you were laughing about last night. If it makes you feel any better, everybody is a little schizophrenic. Normal and abnormal are relative terms which you create according to your preconceived notions about what behavior is considered appropriate at any given time. Take Joan of Arc for example. She heard voices which she claimed were saints and angels talking to her. Considered delusional, mentally imbalanced, and hallucinogenic, she was labeled a heretic and witch and was burned at the stake. Later, she was canonized as a saint."

"Some artists, poets and dreamers are a bit more schizoid than the average person. I think of that book I love *I never promised you a rose garden.* The mentally-ill girl turned inward and created an entire mythic world with gods, characters, and an entire kingdom."

"She was quite brilliant. Again, perceptions and perspectives lie at the heart of all of your behavior. What you believe finds its way into your daily experience and life."

"So is my muse real?"

"Of course she is."

"Are you just a muse?"

"Yes and No. I can be any and all things. I can also come and join you for morning coffee as I have been doing at your kind invitation and leave it to you to decide how real and tangible the experience is. You call it a dream experience. Yet does it not feel real? Can you not taste the wonderful aroma of the coffee even in a dream?"

"I have to admit, it does seem real and I have always felt there is more to dreams than we are aware of."

"I am giving you permission to call me a fictional dream character if that makes you feel better. Call the book you will write fiction. Call it fantasy. Call it a novel. Call it crazy. Just call. People will get out of the book what they need and want. I don't care about facts and fiction. All minor details to me. Real and unreal are two sides of the same coin. Everything you believe is a matter of perception, perspective and emphasis. Well, it's time for me to take my leave. You've got a busy day in front of you. We'll be talking again soon."

Chapter Ten

All That Is

The next morning I woke up at 3 a.m. with the sentence "I am a part of all that is; all that has been and all to be born" repeating itself over and over in my mind. I thought about the little writing it came from, then fell back to sleep. Moments later, my divine guest arrived.

"Hello, Michael. *All That Is* is one of those universal writings that never exhaust themselves or lose meaning or beauty. I would like for you to recite this beautiful poem to me and then let your readers know what brought this writing about."

"Thank you for asking, Mr. Divine. That is my most cherished poem I have ever written. Yes, I have it memorized and am delighted to recite it to you.

All That Is
I am a part of all that is.
All that has been and all to be born.
The spark of life which leads us to this earth
is the same spark giving birth to each morn.

The life force which causes the seed to sprout.
The roses to bud, blossom, and fade
is the same force which set this world in motion.
The moon, the stars, and all planets it made.

This energy is the mother of thought.
The father of courage, goodwill, and love.
It inspires the dreamers who search for more.
and gives beauty to the purest white dove.

The life force takes the eagle to flight.
It gives the sailor his love for the sea.
When the spirit yearns to merge with the all.
it answers the soul's fervent plea.

It permeates the mountains, the hills, the wind.
It directs the tide which forms rolling waves.
It tells the story of life through art
for self expression and creativity it craves.

I am a part of all that is.
All that has been and all to be born.
When the spark of life takes me from this earth.
I shall be greeted by the new morn.

We were quiet for several moments then I spoke. "You asked me to give you the background of this poem. Well, let me see. I was teaching French in a small town high school in southern Indiana. I loved the kids. I loved the small town. I loved working with the track coach and running with the kids after school. I loved co-directing the musical *You're a Good Man, Charlie Brown*. I loved collecting money at the ball games and even fussing at the kids for making out in dark corners at the school dances I chaperoned. It was a year I will never forget. I remember Valentine's Day approaching. I could feel love stirrings in the air. I read love poetry I had written over the years and was filled with glad and sad memories as I recalled my failed relationships and hopes and dreams for love.

"I had not written any love poems in a long time. It was time for a new one, but this time I wanted to write something about a different kind of love other than romantic. After finishing lunch, I headed back to my classroom for my prep period; how I always looked forward to that daily forty-five minutes to myself. In the hallway, I noticed banners announcing the Friday Night Valentine Dance. Big red heart decorations were everywhere. Some lovebirds were sneaking embraces and kisses before the fourth period bell rang. I winked at a couple and shooed them to class, then I closed my door. I noticed that someone had left a little box of valentine heart candy on a back row seat. I examined it and my face lit up with glee as I took out a few pieces of candy, reading little phrases such as Be my valentine, please be mine, I love you, always my Valentine, and so forth. A vivid image of Ginger Ramburger, my first love when I was seven, came to mind; I can still see my face turning red when Ginger kissed me after giving me my Valentine card. I kept that card for years.

"Ah, youth," I sighed. I thought of Frosty the Snowman, the narrator of *Rudolph the Red Nosed Reindeer,* who tells of Rudolph's first day at the reindeer games when he meets the doe Clarice.

"*Yes, young love is sweet,* I thought. Then I returned from my stroll down memory lane and picked up my pen. I spoke to my muse just as plainly and clearly as if she had been standing right in front of me. "Dear muse," I said softly. "Please give me an inspirational writing, but I want one that speaks about a higher love." In my mind, I saw the image of a woman with dark long hair. How I wanted to take her hand and step beyond this world.

To use Dorothy Gayle's wording from *The Wizard of Oz*, I wanted to step beyond the rainbow.

"I heard the words again, "I am a part of All That Is" in my mind. It ended with the sentence "When the spark of life takes me from this Earth, I shall be greeted by the new morn."

"Those two final lines say it all," Mr. Divine said. "Michael, you need to honor your art more. I honor you and your art. If you felt that others believed in and nurtured your art, you would be so much happier. Better still, if you believed in your art and nurtured it more, then others would do likewise. You have carried a deep pain for several lifetimes which is based from a faulty belief that your art is inferior and mediocre. You feel unworthy and undeserving of success. Others told you it was not your place to be the artist; they had their own ideas of who you should be and what roles you should play. There is room for everyone and so many roles to play. Some people are builders. Some are teachers. Some are gardeners. Others are drawn to commerce, technology, philosophy, music, or theology. You are a poet and writer. Your art touches my soul."

"You are telling me that you have a soul? How can God have a soul?"

"If you are a part of all that is, like your writing says, then you are a part of me as well as a part of everyone and everything else. There is soul or life-force present in every living animate as well as inanimate object. I am a living, breathing soul in spite of what some people may think. I have personal and impersonal aspects. Art is a wonderful means to connect with me.

"Unfortunately, not everyone holds this view. Others have not always been supportive or appreciative of your art. As you were put down in this or that life, so you came to put yourself down along with your art. You began to lose more of the sense of who you really were."

"How could that have happened? Doesn't what goes around come around?"

"Yes."

"I must have really been a jerk in some lifetime to be treated so unfairly and disrespectfully."

"A jerk, no. Misinformed and ignorant in some ways, yes."

"I still get sad when I hear that regression tape of that past life where I was not the artist, but a callous hard-working man who did not appreciate or respect art."

"That is not the whole story. I will elaborate on that in a moment, but first I want you to tell your readers about that lifetime."

"What makes you think my readers are going to believe one iota of what I have to say about my exploration of past lives?"

"You might be surprised. More than half of the world believes in reincarnation, and a nice percentage of Westerners believe in it as well."

"Well, if you believe my story might help someone, then I'm up to baring my soul. What have I got to lose? A past life regressionist I used, Sylvia, explained that reading past lives was kind of like watching a movie. She had been trained to read the 'akashic records', which is like a giant strand of etheric energy in the atmosphere that stores the memories of the entire planet and everyone and their experiences upon it. She said that sensitive, trained people can read the vibrations and tune into past life memories. It all sounded fascinating to me as I've always had a pretty open mind. When she asked which lifetime I would like to explore, I simply said I'd like to visit and explore one that impacts and influences me in this lifetime.

"She closed her eyes for a few moments then began talking softly. "I see a man. He is big and burly. His hands are rough and there are some scars and tears on his hands and fingernails. It's obvious that this man works with his hands. He is a builder or what people now call a carpenter. Oh, he has a handsome young son with the most beautiful blue eyes and blond curly hair. His eyes are very sensitive and soulful. This boy is a poet and a painter. Then I move in time, Michael, and I see him and his father arguing. His father is explaining to the boy that painting and poetry cannot bring food in the house or keep a roof over their head. His mother tells the father that her son's poems and paintings bring joy to her soul. The man, who is you, looks at her disdainfully. He then tells his son that he is not welcome in the home anymore.

"The boy takes his meager belongings and heads to a larger city. He goes to what is now Dublin, Ireland. There he meets an older man who takes a liking to him. The man has had a lot more success with his art. He teaches his craft and all he knows to the boy and encourages him, telling him he is very talented. There are a few successes and a year later the boy takes sick with fever. He only lives a few months longer; he has a very loud and deathly cough. The old man wants to take him back to his parents, but he refuses to go, saying he never wishes to see his father again, but would he please give a kiss to his mother.

"The old man honors his wish. When the boy dies, who is now about nineteen years old, the old man puts his body in a wooden casket and draws a horse and carriage and takes him back to the parents. The mother is devastated and the father, you, as well. The old man looks you straight in the eye and says that this boy was the most talented painter he ever had the privilege to know, and he could have become very renowned if circumstances had been different. He made no accusations against you. He spoke to the mother of her son's farewell request and she allowed the old man to kiss her cheeks for her boy.

"You kept the tears back, Michael, but when the old man left, you wept like you never wept before. You would not eat for days; your wife feared you were going to starve yourself. You were never the same again; your guilt ate away at you until it finally led to your demise. What a sad life," Sylvia sighed. "What a bloody sad lifetime."

Mr. Divine's eyes were full of compassion. "Michael, could you relate to that lifetime she spoke of? Did it ring any kind of bell or strike a chord?"

"I felt a big knot in my stomach the whole time Sylvia was talking, and I was engulfed by a terrible sadness. I can believe I lived a lifetime like that. So was my payback from not accepting my artist son to become a poor struggling artist myself?"

"To some degree, yes. After you died, you reevaluated your life as everyone does with their spirit counselors and guides. You agreed to come back and experience what it was like to be in your son's position. You already know about your life in Paris, France as the struggling Impressionist Painter and model. Do you want to talk about that one now?"

"Heavens no, at least not yet. Have I learned my lessons from those two lives yet?"

"What do you think?"

"I know that I am far from being finished with my art. What I found fascinating in another past life reading was that the lady told me I was very creative and artistic. She said it would be very difficult for me in this lifetime to break past those old belief patterns and to restore my self-esteem and belief in my talent. My destiny, she said, was to break the patterns and to create a happy life by earning a good living as a writer. I guess I have quite a ways to go before I am there."

"At least you are trying and you have made progress. My desire is to see you break those old patterns; to see you honor your art and lose yourself in its intensity, beauty and passion without thinking you are going over the edge into madness."

"I do have a fear of madness, don't I?"

"Yes, an old one which goes very deep. But you are not here to go mad in this lifetime. You nearly did that in your last one and a few before. It is time to heal, grow, and move on. It grieves my heart to see people suffer. Emotional suffering can be as bad, if not worse, than physical suffering. I look forward to the day when you and everyone will allow yourselves to be fully human and fully alive.

"For you, part of being 'fully alive' involves expressing yourself creatively via the written word and music."

"I agree."

"The love inside you is very big. It wants to expand and reach out and touch all of life just as the plants reach for the sunlight. Your unhappiness and fears curtail that far too much. You said, 'You are a part of all that is. All that has been and all to be born.' Take it a step further. Don't just acknowledge it intellectually. Feel and let yourself know it experientially. You fear your passions and have tried most of your life to quell them."

"A lady once told me that is why I always stop the flow of my writing. She said I go places and feel things so intensely that it's almost too much for me. I back off because I get overwhelmed."

"There is a place for being overwhelmed. What is happening is that your heart and emotions are being stretched and expanded so you can take in more love. I can assure you that life and love do not wish to hurt you in any way. Love never does. It is fear that hurts and limits you. Michael, it is time to move past fear. Love is the greatest gift you can offer to anyone, including yourself."

"I know."

"It is time to write about love. Sing about it. Love, love. Love life and let love and life love you in return. The angels rejoice each time people let love saturate their being and then move it outwards to all life. You will cease feeling that gnawing void and emptiness the moment you stop denying who you are and start be-ing who you are."

"Next you are going to advocate hugging trees and everyone you run into."

"What is wrong with that?"

"Well, I think Dr. Leo Buscaglia has already earned the title The Love, or is it The Hug Doctor, or both?"

"I guarantee that if you hugged as many people as he has, you'd never be depressed."

"Isn't he just a bit too much? And yet I waited in line for an hour to get one of his full-body hugs when I heard him speak in California."

"How did it make you feel?"

"I have to admit I enjoyed it, though part of me felt awkward for hugging a stranger."

"Let me remind you of what Leo Buscaglia knows deep down, and what you need to remember. We just talked about this in your writing where you say 'I am a part of all that is. All That has been and all to be born.' Given this fact then, there can be no strangers."

"I know this in my heart of hearts. I guess we all need to be reminded."

"That is partly what my job entails. I am here to re-mind you. To help reset your mind if you will."

"Want to know something? You make a great, preacher and teacher, Mr. Divine."

"I will take that as a compliment and give you one as well. You also are a good teacher. We've had a nice time this morning, haven't we? Well, I think I'll be taking my leave now.

Chapter Eleven

The War Child
Soldier in Contemplation

I had no visits from Mr. Divine the next week, but he promptly showed up the following Monday dressed in a GI Joe type of army green outfit and black leather boots. I wondered if we were going to talk about war today. Boot camp. Grunts. Machine guns. Weapronry. Kids playing with toy guns. That never appealed to me. It all makes my stomach queasy.

"What are we going to talk about today?" I asked him after we engaged in some light conversation.

"We are going to change the pace in this visit. We are going to talk about what is sometimes referred to as trapped earthbound souls. To set the tone, let's begin by talking about Heaven. Heaven is a peaceful place where those souls go after death whose awareness is aligned with positive vibrations. It is my wish that everyone go there after making the transition commonly known as death. It is important to not leave this world filled with anger, bitterness, and hurt for you truly do take it with you; it actually determines where you go. If you die at peace with yourself, the people in your world, and the world at large, you will go to a peaceful place after you pass on. Unfortunately, many people do not die at peace with themselves or with other people in their lives. Some souls are so filled with anger, hurt, and darkness that they simply do not know how to go to Heaven or perhaps to the light is a better word. Such souls get stuck between heaven and Earth. The girl in your writing *The War Child* is about an earthbound soul who is trapped between two realms."

I gulped and gasped. "You know about the girl in *The War Child?*"

"Are we pushing buttons here?" Mr. Divine asked.

"You might say that. That is a very personal and haunting writing. Do we have to talk about it? Can't we let the poor, dead girl rest?"

"Not when she doesn't know she is dead, which is what she needs to know so that she can rest."

"So are you going to tell me she is lost in space, kind of like that old TV show?"

"In a way she is. *The War Child* shows that life after death can be as bad or worse than life before death. You may not be aware of it, but you have stepped through the illusion of time and space and met the war child."

I gulped again. "I am not sure I am ready for this."

"Of course you are, Mr. Divine" replied, matter of factly, "you have been haunted by that mysterious little writing for years. Now is the time for the mystery to be solved. I would like for you to fill the reader in on the background of what inspired your war writings."

"I will try, but this is a very sensitive area with me. I wrote *The War Child* along with two other pieces in 1988. In addition to my teaching job, and being involved with several extracurricular activities along with my daily jogging and reading, I was also doing some writing. I recall watching the TV mini-series *War and Remembrance* where Jane Seymoor played a leading role as a holocaust victim.

"I had seen holocaust movies before, but for some reason, that TV mini-series did a number on me. *War and Remembrance* was affecting me strongly in ways I could not understand. The title especially haunted me. I called a friend and she suggested that I might try to give voice to my thoughts through writing."

"Is there a single line or two that stands out from the war 'writings?'"

"Yes," I said, softly. "Two: Hope is buried beside the dead. And Is there no hope for the human race? War is disgusting. What a disgrace!" Those lines are from another little writing that I lost. But those lines I have never forgotten.

Mr. Divine was looking at me with the kindest expression on his face. Seeing him sitting there so cool, calm and collected in his GI Joe outfitwhile I felt like a seething madman, made me feel like I had just stepped into a virtual reality movie. I took some deep breaths and slowly began to calm down.

"Let yourself experience the feelings that are coming up?" Mr. Divine said gently. "A lot of old memories are being awakened here. They need to come up. How did your story come about?"

During that week I watched the TV war mini-series, I started having dreams about this little girl. She was stumbling along a deserted street among the debris and the dead. She sees her mother lying on the ground, blood pouring from her mouth and cries for her to get up. Tears fall down her face as ominous winds slap at her face. She keeps wandering back and forth down this one street, wailing in desperation as she sees so many helpless dead victims.

"The images of the little girl were so vivid that it felt like I was there with her, although I had no idea where there was. When I woke up, I found myself pacing back and forth, almost with the same stride as the little girl. 'She has no one to talk to. No one to sing her melodies which bring her joy,' I recall saying out loud. 'She has no one to tell her that this must only be a dream.' I would try to forget about her, but every night for the rest of the *War and Remembrance* mini-series I dreamed of her. How I wanted to reach out to her. How I wanted to wipe away the tears streaming down her cold red cheeks. How I wanted to take her in my arms and assure her that everything would be alright. 'She deserves a better life,' I would say. Won't someone take her from this desolate land?

"The last night I dreamed of her, she was walking slower down the street with her head hanging down. I woke up with that image in my mind and with tear filled eyes, I wrote in my journal, 'The war child walks on with no where to go in her dismal world of war and strife.' Then I knew the men in the white coats were coming for me. The dreams ended, but never the memories. To try to come to grips with the powerful emotions the mini-series and dreams generated, I wrote a story which I'm sorry to say got lost in between one of my many moves.

"*The War Child* haunts me as much now as it did the day I wrote it some seventeen years ago. I found myself at odd times staring into space, glassy eyed, lost and feeling totally helpless to assist this poor little girl, whoever and wherever she was. I had told myself for years that she was just an imaginary person I had created out of my own loneliness and need for company. Still, she haunted me. I talked about her to a few friends and I even went on the Internet and shared the story with total strangers, tears pouring down my cheeks. I could not believe that I had asked total strangers to help me find this little girl. They must have thought I was a real nut case. She somehow took a life of her own beyond the dreams and even the memories because I could never forget about her. I'd go for days or weeks without thinking about her and then out of the blue, it would all come back. Sometimes, I thought I even felt her presence though I told myself that must surely be impossible."

We were quiet a few moments then Mr. Divine spoke. "Michael, the war child's pain calls out to you. Through the miles and through the stretch of time and space she reaches out to you."

"How can she do that? I don't even know if she is real or not?"

"She is very real; she is just not alive on the same plane and dimension that you are. Like I said before, this is a soul that is trapped between two worlds. She does not believe she is dead, and she will listen to no one who tries to tell her that she is."

"I should call my friend Victoria. Helping to free earth-bound spirits is right up her alley."

"She does not care to meet Victoria. She is your case."

"The only case I think I need now is a case of very strong ale to numb and help me forget about that poor child."

"You cannot forget about this child."

"How can this be happening to me? I was feeling so great earlier – so calm and serene and now this."

"Now this. Welcome to life on the Earth. You are an

emotional person. You are an Empath. You have always been able to easily pick up on the moods and feelings of others. Since you are also a clairvoyant and medium, you are able to perceive energies and souls of people, not only on the Earth residing in human bodies, but also souls who are no longer inhabiting physical bodies. You are like a wide open receiver and antenna if you will. Other parts of you are constantly exploring the regions of space and the spirit world. You encounter and meet many souls in your night time dream excursions. In this respect, the war child is no stranger to you.

"You have a maternal nurturing side and this is what draws her to you. Humans broadcast their emotions and their true character like radio signals in the ether and atmosphere. Sensitive people can pick up the waves much like a radio frequency. Sensitive spirits can do the same thing, actually much easier than most people, since they are no longer encumbered by the physical body. Since there is no time or space, you can move from any moment to another and be back right where you started within moments or even less; more like micro-seconds or quantum leaps as some refer to it. You are learning that I am but a thought away. Although you doubt at times, you are beginning to really look forward to our visits, are you not?"

"Yes."

"I am considered by most people to be a very long distance from here. Heaven, as they reckon it, is even further away than the rainbow or the edge of the sky, or the very Earth itself. You are learning to project your consciousness at lightning paces of speed. Thought certainly moves faster than the speed of light. Everyone has a story to tell how they thought of someone and heard from that person that very moment, whether via a phone call, letter, email, what have you. They were communicating on a higher frequency. Telepathy is far more common than you might think; it is especially powerful between a mother and her child, and especially her unborn child. This is why it is so important for a mother to be subjected to as little stress as possible during her pregnancy. She and the unborn child are symbiotically linked very deeply, and both know on a soul level what the other is feeling and experiencing. A child can be marred and damaged for life if his or her mother undergoes extreme emotional trauma during her pregnancy."

"I can believe that. I am convinced that my baby brother, Bradley, underwent such damage. Mom was an alcoholic and was horribly abused by my father throughout the pregnancy. He'd tell her he wished she and the baby would die, and he was constantly cursing at her, and beating her. It's a miracle that she or the baby survived all of that."

"A tragedy that occurs much too frequently."

"I am still not over his tragic death in 1997 at the young age of 27."

"Your brother is with you far more often than you realize. You do visit in dream time and you will meet again in a future lifetime. At least he made it to the light and is in a good place. The poor war child is trapped. It is her own fear that enslaves her, but she is trapped nonetheless."

"Can't you do anything?"

"I have sent you to help her. My light would overwhelm and scare her, but yours will not. If you can remember that there is no time or space or separation of any kind, you will be more able to reach out and respond to her. You need not see her on the physical plane to be able to help her."

"I know. Victoria tells me that a lot. But I'm still too scared to go to her. Traveling through time and space, even which you say does not exist, may be but a moment or a thought away, but I can't rush into anything I am not ready for."

"I understand. I just wanted to give you some insight on what is going on with the war child. You will be able to help her in time. You already do in dream time, I might add."

"Thank you. I will send her prayers, love and healing light, and when I feel ready and capable, I will try to go to her and attempt to set her free even though I am not sure how to do that."

"Your soul will know just what to do. Now we are ready to hear your other war writing, *Soldier in Contemplation*. I have much to say about it, but first let's hear it. I know it is another that you have memorized."

"Yes, it is."

Mr. Divine shifted positions and placed his hands in his lap, his eyes focused intently on me. I trembled slightly. I made myself comfortable, took a couple of deep breaths and spoke.

Soldier in Contemplation

Dear God,

Will I ever understand war? How people justify destroying what is sacred. We are all equal in your eyes. You gave us the breath of life, and we take life in the name of greed and preserving peace. Young men not in the prime of life are forced to fulfill someone else's dreams which are given birth in the pits of Hell.

Fiery passionate obsessions of war haunt the mind and torment the soul. How can anyone ask us to extinguish the human spark of God? Birth is a marvel we should cherish. Life should be honored, for does not our God dwell deep in the heart, and chambers of the soul? Our captains exhort us to fight these wars to be free from the awesome foe. Onward we march in patriotic duty like barbarian warriors fully prepared to kill.

Perhaps the battle will be won, but we will never be free. Nightmarish horrors of those deathly moments will be embedded in our soul and memories for the rest of our lives. We won't know the real from the insane.

Perhaps this reality is insane and we who partake of war are no better than those we allow to dictate our destinies. When will we learn, dear God?

War is cruel, absurd and humiliating. Please God, let me rest in peace!

Tears were streaming down my cheeks. I thought I noticed one dripping down Mr. Divine's as well. We were quiet for a few moments. I was lost in silent contemplation of a phenomenon I would never understand.

"I keep seeing a blurry image of a dark haired young man writing this letter," I said.

Mr. Divine looked at me for several moments as though

weighing how to explain something. Then he moved a bit closer and spoke softly. "Michael, that letter to God was written from the heart of a sensitive soldier."

"You mean I didn't just make it up?"

He shook his head no. I didn't like where this conversation was headed.

"Take a deep breath. What I am about to tell you is probably going to rock your world to use one of your sayings."

"That is one of my friend Victoria's sayings, too. Well, I guess I am ready to get my world rocked, but I get goose bumps wondering what you will say next. The thought just sends chills up and down my spine and makes my stomach churn."

Mr. Divine scooted a little closer to me. "Michael, *Soldier in Contemplation* has always haunted you because it is personal to you in a way you have never been able to explain, but you have always felt it. Every time you read the letter, you can identify with that soldier and feel a sense of kinship with him."

"I do and I am always filled with despair and desperation."

"Do you recall that dream you had a few days after writing it?"

"Yes, I have never forgotten it. In the dream, I was in an old house in a bedroom looking in a big oval mirror. Slowly, my features began shifting. The experience scared me so I jumped back. Then I heard a noise. Someone was coming upstairs. Before I could run away, this man stepped into the room. He was dressed in a soldier's outfit. I could see him very clearly – that is, all but his face. I asked him who he was. He very slowly walked towards me. He pointed at the mirror. We both approached it. When I looked inside the mirror, my face was concealed. I looked at the man and he was wearing my face. Frightened, I let out a cry, then I woke up from the dream. I never had it again."

"That was because it was too confrontational for you. Michael, that dream was more than a dream. That man who came to you was one of your past life selves. You were the soldier, Michael, and the writing is the letter you wrote before you took your own life. You had had it with war and killing and decided that the life of a soldier was not a life you wanted to live. You were fed up even though there was a lot of pressure put on the young men to serve their country and do their military duty to help protect the homeland. You could not face the possibility that you would survive the war and have to live with the memories for the rest of your life. So you ended your life at the age of twenty-four. Your soul and subconscious know that and you remember; ergo the reason why the show *War and Remembrance* haunts you so much."

I was shaking like a leaf. I tried to speak, but nothing came out but a half audible squeak. We were quiet for a long time. I wanted to scream the word impossible, but I couldn't even utter a whisper let alone speak or scream. Some time later, I cleared my throat and found that I could talk again.

"No wonder the *War and Remembrance* mini-series affected me so deeply," I said softly. "You know something else. I've always known in this life that war was not for me. When I was in the eighth grade we wrote letters to the North Vietnamese government in Hanoi asking them to release the American POWs. My letter was the longest and most emphatic one of all the students in the class. My History teacher said that if any of the letters could move the hearts of the North Vietnamese that mine would. The war ended a few months later and I didn't have to sign up for the draft. I just knew that I would never go to war. I might be a Cryptologist, a translator, a cook or a jester to entertain the troops, but I'd never pick up a gun and fight. I have always disliked guns in this life and have never owned one.

"That was a sad life, Michael, but the good news is that to quote your last line, 'Dear God, please let me rest in peace!' you were able to rest in peace. Your guides helped disengage your spirit from your body and you were immediately taken to one of the hospitals in the spirit world. You were not judged as no soul is judged. One thing you learned from that lifetime is that suicide is not the answer to life's problems no matter how difficult or overwhelming they can be. When you sit in counsel with your guides on the other side, you always examine your intention behind your actions. You did not commit suicide out of fear, hatred, nor the desire to escape some hidden guilt or crime. You truly valued and cherished life and you were appalled to be expected to take life – life that you felt was precious and not yours to take. Your good karma in this lifetime was not to have to be involved with war at all. That suicide life was not in vain, but it is not one to repeat."

"I've always felt that. There have been many times that I wanted to end my life hoping the pain would go away. But in my heart, I've always known that suicide is not the answer."

"You bring some of that soul knowing back from your soldier life."

"Thank you. So what about my other writings? Are they past life memories as well? I will never forget that time my friend Janet and I were meditating together listening to this very captivating CD. I felt myself going into some kind of trance or something. Suddenly in my mind's eye I saw a young man and a woman skipping in a field. I knew they were deeply in love and I also knew that he was part black but did not know it. Learning who he really was, was going to change his life forever. I told Janet about it and she encouraged me to write my thoughts down. It became a short story."

"Yes, that was a past life that you lived, but not all characters in stories were you in your past lives. Some can be the past lives of other people you know or do not know. Some are remnants of past life experiences that you spice up using your imagination where truth and fantasy intermingle. If you look beyond the words and the images that the words portray, you will discover that there is much more hidden meanings to stories than people realize."

"I can see how it can become very mind boggling."

"Well, part of my job is to help unboggle (my new word for the day) all of this," Mr. Divine said.

"Well, I'm all for unboggling."

Mr. Divine grinned. "Yes, although you are already asleep, this has all been very intense. You need some uninterrupted sleep."

"Yes, I think I've had enough for one day, especially when this feels more real than being awake. I know I'll remember all of this."

I slept for three more hours. When I got up, I was in a daze. That had been the most intense visit with Mr. Divine ever. I thought about the war writings for several days. I recalled my visit to the American cemetery in Normandy, France when I studied in France. I tried to examine every headstone and catch every name. My professor had to yell at me several times to join the group. I could have spent the entire day in that cemetery. I recalled visiting Germany and talking to different people about the wars. I recalled working at two Jewish summer resorts and how affected and upset I became when I saw numbers tattooed on some of the people's arms.

I recalled a record my foster sister gave me when I was fourteen years old. I could still hear those plaintive haunting words, "What do you win when you win a war? You win nothing." I listened to that record more times than I could count. I remembered the Christmas movie I had bought years ago *I'll be home for Christmas* about a family's young son off to war who never comes home. It upset me so much, I could never watch it again. I have quite a collection of war movies. Mr. Divine had definitely touched a chord.

To think that spirits trapped between two worlds could step through time and reach out for help was a bit mind boggling, but it somehow hit a deep chord in my being. I had always known there was more involved than my imagination when I wrote *The War Child* piece. The experience had affected me too strongly. And to think that one of my own past life selves had stepped through time to give me a letter I had written as a past life soldier was also mind boggling, but somehow made sense. There is so much we don't know. So much to learn.

I wondered what other surprises and insights I would receive from Mr. Divine. Was I getting into something way over my head? My heart said no. I have always been a thinker who likes to ponder the depths of the soul. The superficial answers that most people accept about life and its mysteries have never appealed to me. Most people are not even intelligent enough to ask the deeper questions. I silently gave gratitude and mentally told Mr. Divine how I looked forward to our next visit.

Chapter Twelve

Glimpse

A few days later I woke up thinking about something I had written many years ago titled *Glimpse*. It resulted from a yearning I have had all of my life to behold the form of God, whatever that could possibly be. I was about to get up and go search for it, but a drowsiness hit me and the next thing I knew I was fast asleep. I wondered if my divine guest had something to do with that because moments later he appeared.

"Good morning, Michael. You've sure been pondering some deep mysteries as of late."

Mr. Divine cocked his head forward and looked at me with his penetrating, glowing eyes. I instantly became giddy as I always get lost in his radiant blue eyes. I felt that if I gazed at him even seconds more, I'd melt into star dust and disappear into nothingness. I quickly looked away.

"So you want to know what I look like? Before I respond to that question, I'd like to hear *Glimpse*. Inspirational writing often describes what ordinary speech can barely approximate. You pretty well sum things up in that one. I think it is one of your best. Before reciting it, will you do the honors again and give some background for the reader's information?"

"I think I have been waiting all of my life to write *Glimpse*. From the time I was very young, I was fascinated with the idea of beholding the face of God. The story in *The Bible* of Moses and the burning bush has always intrigued me. My eyes would get all big as I read about Moses asking God who he was, and God replying, 'I am that I am,' and he basically told Moses to look away because to behold his form would burn him to a crisp.

"The idea of the finite beholding the infinite goes way back with me. As a kid, I was determined to see God. I believed and felt in my little boy heart of hearts that God was kind and real, and I was filled with a yearning to look at him face to face. I'd look at the pictures of Jesus in church and other places and lose myself, and I wanted to see God.

"I remember when I was four years old when we lived in a big white house on a hill in Belmont, Kentucky. There was a little wooded area behind our house where I used to wander. There I'd talk to God. I also talked to the squirrels, the birds and to my many invisible and imaginary friends, as well. I remember that I'd turn this or that log over hoping to find a clue as to where God might be hiding from me. I'd look behind trees, in ditches, in creeks and hope that God would smile at me over my shoulder. I looked any and everywhere I could find to look. I even looked in an old cedar chest at my grandmother's and in the dank dark closets upstairs to see if God might be hiding there.

"Like the two characters in the Samuel Beckett play *Waiting for Godot,* I guess I was also waiting for God to show up. Like in the play, he never did, but I never gave up. As I grew older and my intellect blossomed, I began to entertain the idea that to behold God's image would not be like seeing another person face to face. There must be more to God than a human portrait could possibly portray.

"Several years ago, I had a strange dream where I was in a room full of mirrors of all sizes and shapes with a voice thundering overhead. I immediately looked up and was taken in by the masculine strong voice that was speaking words I could not make out. I was very attracted by the booming power in that voice, although it was very strong, it still felt benevolent to me. The mirrors began to tilt towards me and each one made a little musical tinkling sound as it turned. I began examining each one in hopes of discovering what lay behind it. Perhaps God was playing hide and seek with me.

"When I got to the last mirror, I saw a little button in the middle, slightly above my neck which said push. I pushed the button and the mirror became a portal that opened. I stepped inside to the blackest void I had ever seen before. I could not even see my finger in front of me. I tried to let out a yelp, but found I was voiceless. I finally managed one word, "Help," then

I awoke. That dream was very unsettling to me. I felt that the portal and the blackness were some kind of clue. What lay behind that void? And why did I wake up? I wanted to go back to sleep and finish that dream more than I have ever wanted to return to a dream.

"I started whispering three words, 'take me back.' As I repeated it over and over in a little sing song chanting voice, I began putting myself into some kind of hypnotic trance. I became drowsy, then drifted off to sleep. But the dream did not return. When I awoke a few minutes later, I had a strong urge to write. *Glimpse* is what came forth. I was so impressed and moved by it that I immediately memorized it," I said then recited.

Glimpse

Whence originates this yearning to behold the face of God? Do I really believe these mortal eyes could behold such luminescence? Would so much light engulf me and annihilate me, or would it perhaps burn through my mortality until it reached the seed of my soul? Can the soul be perceived and felt with senses unscathed by mortal form? Can transcendental love and celestial realms, which poetry and song attempt to unveil, dwell deep within my soul?"

Are there clues which can help me discover the realms of the Immortals? Are the whispers of the muses more than dreamy tones of fancy? Can the voices who sing in my dreams soothe me with divine music when night sleeps? I hear no answers to these questions, but I feel a sense of peace and joyful anticipation. Soon, my longings shall know rest. My wandering mind serves me well, leading me to the golden, immortal gates.

The search is nearly over. Innocence opens the door for me there to behold the face of God. I slowly open my eyes and approach an oval mirror where I behold written in silver, the word, LOVE. I step inside then question no more!

We were both quiet for several moments, then Mr. Divine spoke.

"The answer to your question is simple. My essence is love.

When you step beyond your limited finite mortal thinking and acknowledge your *true* essence, then you will acknowledge mine as well. You will then realize that I am 'everything,' so I look like everything. I can take on any appearance and don any form I choose, wear any mask or outfit I desire. As you learn to see with untainted vision, you will behold the unadulterated beauty that lies behind every form and know that it is all part and parcel of who I am. And equally important, it is part of who you are."

I wanted to ask if God is also the demon that tries to possess an innocent child, the murderer that kills ruthlessly, the bank robber, the rapist, and so on. But I could not. I was speechless. Nothing mattered right now. Nothing was more important than "this moment." I wanted it to last forever. It was magical. It was miraculous. No matter that this was all a dream. I was standing in the presence of the Almighty. It was real to me. Mr. Divine smiled at me and reached out for my hand. I wanted to bask in His presence forever!

Chapter Thirteen

Your World is Your World

I woke up one morning in early March with Christmas songs on my mind. After breakfast, I went to my computer room which I also call The North Pole (as I keep it decorated all year long), and was filled with more Christmas spirit. In my mind, I kept hearing Elvis Presley singing *Why can't everyday be like Christmas?* I noticed a box in the corner which had colorful holiday posters in it. The next thing I knew I was down on my knees trimming the posters and taping them on the walls. "This is so goofy," I said, feeling a little self conscious – this keeping Christmas decorations up all year. I am a kook."

The next morning my divine guest showed up dressed in a red robe. He was wearing a Christmas hat with the white ball on top. I found it amusing and could not hold back my snickers. He burst out into a huge grin then let out a big, "Ho Ho Ho. So you think you are a kook. Everyone is a little kooky, Michael. Remember, it is all a matter of perspective and perception. What you believe is real for you and the same goes for everyone else."

"It just feels silly to be putting up more Christmas decorations in March."

"Only if you think so."

"I should be taking things down, not adding. Mom thinks I'm half nuts when I tell her what I'm up to. And yet the poor woman is on so many pills. Anti depressants. Sleeping pills. Anxiety pills and all the ones for her medical conditions."

"Think about it. Your world is your world. Your Christmas room serves many purposes for you. It is a sanctuary where you can step into your inner realms any time you desire. As you have learned, there are countless probable worlds in existence simultaneously and 'other yous' are actively involved in them in many different time periods. As you expand your consciousness, you can learn to perceive some of these probable selves and realities. Your natural sense of magic and wonder is very real and important to you. It keeps life interesting and a bit mysterious. Everyone needs some wonder and mystery in their life. I could take you on visits to many worlds that are lit up in bright lights all the time. You are aware of some of these worlds on deeper levels and that is one reason you love having your North Pole Christmas room decorated all year.

"A sanctuary can be anywhere, and it can be the springboard to take you anywhere on your inner journeys as well. Bright colors and the Santa motif resonate to you, so you have chosen that theme for your sanctuary."

"Well, actually I have others as well: My angel room sanctuary, my fairy sanctuary, for example."

"Some people prefer the summer. You love summer, but you also love winter and autumn and spring."

"Yes. Just the other day, I was picking up some of the glittering snow off the floor. I wished I had more snow for my little winter wonderland scene. I happened to look in this box and there was a half bag left. There was a glittering scene with Santa and his reindeer flying above a big church steeple with a full white moon in the background. It was so magical. Underneath were the words: 'Add some sparkle to enhance your village and winter scenes.' I sprinkled the rest of the snow on my winter scenes and I imagined myself right there."

"You just said a key word – imagine. What you can imagine, you can create. You are all co-creators with me. What you believe and see is what you get. We are all in this grand adventure together. Isn't it grand?"

"Yes. So what we see is what we get."

"Exactly. What you see is what you get. And what you believe is what you see."

"I wrote a fantasy story, *The Secret of Magic,* some years ago which said that it's the believing that leads to the seeing, not the other way around."

"That was a profound revelation that people need to hear over and over. Your little home mini-version of the North Pole is based on your belief that magic, wonder, and the sparkle and joy of Christmas are natural and can be enjoyed everyday, not just one predetermined day of the year. The physical manifestation and creation is but a mere reflection of a belief. On a much larger scale, that is the secret of creation. Let me add that I do like your Christmas sanctuary. It reflects some deep seated beliefs you have come to incorporate into your life.

"You are getting past the cultural idea that life is meant to be a struggle; that you have to work by the sweat of your brow until you retire or until you croak, to use one of your humorous words. You are indeed working, or shall I say playing, with the idea that you can make sufficient amounts of money in short periods of time."

"My friend Leiah calls it working smart, not hard. It's about time that I try a different approach after so many years of struggling day to day to get by, let alone week to week like most people do. Scrimping and scraping is for the birds. It's sad how so many people live from paycheck to paycheck. I'm embarrassed to admit it, but for years I did much worse than that. After I quit teaching in 1990, I lived from day to day for several years, even into my mid forties. It's embarrassing because I have some wealthy friends."

"That so many people live from paycheck to paycheck saddens my heart as well. How I rejoiced when you decided you were going to move past your poverty consciousness and you set out on a journey to do just that. The journey to success begins with the first step. Every change begins with the intention to change. You have read books. You have attracted people who know how to make a lot of money and who understand solid business principles and the Universal Law of Attraction that is being talked about so much now. They have been coaching you. I give you credit; you have been a good student and are still learning. The universal Law of Attraction is very simple. When total belief is there and you back it up with emotion, you attract anything you desire. So watch what you ask for. You are getting better. Practice makes perfect. Remember your successes and not your failures. With each success, come new ones.

"You believe in magic and miracles and your little home mini North Pole is a visual reflection of that. Your clients love your Christmas room. They say it makes them feel childlike and magical."

"Yes, I am getting quite the reputation as 'the North Pole Man' as some call me. I even have clients bringing me Christmas decorations. I cherish them."

"People may think it peculiar that someone keeps their lights up all year, and there are more people who do that than you might realize."

"Keeping their lights up is one thing, but what about having your entire living room lit up with not a nook or a cranny uncovered with posters, Christmas dolls, music boxes, strings of lights galore, wreaths, garland, bulbs, candles, you name it. I have snowflakes everywhere and miniature trees and who knows what else. Isn't that going overboard a bit?"

"It is all personal preference. Some people know the words to two or three songs. Others know ten. Still others know dozens. You simply fit in the dozens category. We were talking about sanctuaries. What you believe and hold to be true in your inner world (the world of your thoughts, beliefs and feelings), determines what makes its way and manifests in the outer one. Some people realize this. Others do not, but they shall in time. Your inner world has always been important to you, so do not be so eager to challenge it. It has been your refuge many times when the outer world has been simply too unbearable. Your faith and spontaneity and belief in angels and the inner realms brought you an actual encounter with an angel which changed your life. Your angel lit and ignited the spark of hope at a very dark time of your young life. You chose to believe what she said. Then you attracted to yourself the very positive changes that she saw coming in your life. This is how it works.

"Rejoice and be happy about your inner sanctuary. You light up my life. You really do. You are delightful. Full of light. The essence of your soul and true being is pure undiluted light. This is why your pal Sarah told you that since we are not who we think we are, it does not matter which names we use. One of the lessons for many people in this lifetime is to stop worrying and giving undue attention to what others think of them. The best way to get rid of negativity is to ignore it as much as you can. Often that in itself is enough to drive it away. But not always. Sometimes you have to take different measures and choose which confrontations are appropriate.

"I am here to tell you that your mini North Pole is beautiful. It inspires and fills you with joy and delight. That is what Christmas is about. It fills you with a yearning to become a part of the light you see around you. This is all good. For someone else, their sanctuary is created around other themes. To many men, their sanctuary revolves around sports images. They have pictures of their favorite sports heroes about. There might be an autographed picture, a bat, a baseball, a basketball or a football. There may be other paraphernalia such as big blasting TVs where they hoop and holler over the Super Bowl and other games while they drink beer and eat pizza. These fellows love the competition and the competitive spirit that sports gives them. To other men, it is the hunting theme. They have their stuffed buck head hanging over their fireplace and show it off proudly. They may have a fancy gun case where they keep their prized rifles and guns which they polish and clean diligently. My advice to you and to everyone is to follow your bliss. It is not always important to know why you are drawn to something or someone. Your soul has its own reasons which you are often not consciously aware of."

"Don't our past lives influence who and what we are drawn to?"

"Yes, but let me remind you that some of you move past your lives and step beyond them to the realms of spirit. Some of what you are drawn to can be due to an experience you had in between lives or even before you experienced your first life in human form. Since time does not exist, it is but a moment ago that you were sparks of pure undulating light dancing across the stars and galaxies. As I have said before, the true essence of your being and soul is light. Your soul body and form are light bodies so it is not surprising that some of you are so drawn to light. For example, did not Jesus say, 'I am the light of the world?' And he was just that. Although he was speaking metaphorically, there was also some literal truth involved. As you move into pure goodness and unconditional love, your body actually lightens up. Your aura or energy field brightens and becomes a pure golden white light the more you evolve. This is why you see halos around saints in the paintings of the Middle Ages.

"I know that you love bright colored lights. You are not sure why other than to say that colored lights make you feel cheerful and good as well as stir up longings and yearnings. I will tell another reason for your yearnings and attraction to the lights. On a soul level, you are recalling journeys you make in spirit time to places and realms that are lit up in the most brilliant lights you could ever imagine. There are places where it is the Fourth of July every single day. Every single minute, I might add. You know on a deep level that you and the light are one. To look at the beautiful bright colors fills your heart and soul with gladness and reminds you of this deep truth. You shall probably have lights strung up no matter where you live. Other people like to light candles or enjoy the light and warmth of a fireplace. Again, the soul is drawn to light, for light is its true essence and as you know, the light cannot exist or be perceived in the absence of darkness. In the next chapter, I propose that we explore the darkness in more depth."

"I'm all for that. The darkness used to terrify me, but not anymore. Now, I cannot even sleep well if I'm not in the dark. I honor and salute both the light and the darkness and make a toast to them both."

"I second that," Mr. Divine said as he waved his hand. Two glasses of sparkling champagne appeared and we made a toast, then he bade me adieu and took his leave.

Chapter Fourteen

Fear, Embrace Me No More

It was a week before my divine guest showed up again. He seemed to know when I had other obligations that needed tending to. Things began settling down over the next few days and the following Monday I woke up before dawn from an unsettled dream. I quickly wrote down what I remembered. I would ask Mr. Divine about it. He must have heard my request because the next morning, he showed up promptly for our dream visit. I put on a robe and headed downstairs. Mr. Divine was staring intently at the fireplace. He was wearing a red sweatpants outfit with a black bandana and black jogging shoes. His shiny, golden hair was hanging over his shoulders.

"Well, good morning, Mr. Divine. You up for some coffee?"

"Of course. Your coffee is always so delectable"

"Give me a few minutes. Any special request?"

"Surprise me."

A few minutes later Mr. Divine and I were both making slurping noises as we sipped our mocha coffee. The twinkle and glow was in his eyes as usual. His demeanor was calm and relaxed. He looked at me deeply with compassion and pure unconditional love. His eyes looked both youthful and old; perhaps ancient is the proper word. What impressed me is how engaging his eyes were. Not only his eyes, but every part of him. He has this way of making you feel like you are the most important person in the world to him.

After we went in the living room and settled down comfortably, he said, "I thought that today we would talk about the darkness."

"The other day we talked about my sanctuary and me being a big kid at heart who has to have Christmas lights up all year. You told me why I love having colored lights strung up all year.

I guess today is the day to take the elevator down and step into the darkness."

"Elevator going down."

"Thank goodness I am no longer afraid of the dark. Well, that's not completely true. Guess I should say for the most part. The darkness I fear the most is my inner darkness."

"We are not going to step into the darkness today; we are just going to talk about it."

"So how do we begin talking about the darkness?"

"You start."

"Well let me see, I have felt settled and peaceful the past few days. Then I got a few emails from someone which depressed me. It seems when life starts to get good and we begin to feel in the flow, that the damn, excuse my French because I'm frustrated, dark side comes after us. It reminds me of some horror movie I saw where this voodoo priest would say, 'The darkness come a callin.' It's like some neon light goes out to the universe and says, 'This one is beginning to feel good about himself. Life is getting good. He's getting in the flow. He's having too much fun. It's time for a little drama and trauma.' Is that how it is? Are we doomed to not have any peace of mind for any extended amount of time?"

"Not at all. You are actually given the opportunity to choose more of it or to choose trauma and setbacks."

"Well, the temporary peace of mind was sure nice while it lasted."

"Do not be so faint of heart. It is coming back. I assure you. You are all, everyone, just setting up for yourself a few tests to see what you really want and the opportunity to clear away and move through some of your inner darkness. You are not free from the Earth until a fair amount of your inner darkness is cleared and merged with the light."

"I see. It does seem that every time I start to get in the flow and feel good about myself, something throws me off kilter."

"Maybe it is time to look at the situations around you and see what they mean since everything has meaning. You are in a position to notice and discover the meanings that exist in your everyday circumstances when you are in that half-dream, half-awake state of mind before getting up."

"I had this dream the other night. I remember feeling much more lucid afterwards. Every thing seemed to have meaning; even the objects around me. I remember looking up at my new rose clock and thinking, this time I will get it right. Then I was drawn to the little tick tock noise the clock made and I thought, let them who can hear, hear. Intuition speaks so don't shut it out like the tick tock of the clock that ceased a few moments when the battery fell out the other day. I remember putting the battery back in and my senses seemed to be heightened."

"They were. You are very sensitive, Michael; much more than the average person. This makes you a natural empath and 'absorber,' my new word for you today. You absorb much more than you are consciously aware. All of your moods are not yours. Sometimes you are simply taking in and absorbing the moods and feelings of others; especially those you have strong connections with. More people are heightening their sensitivity. This fills them with more love and compassion for each other, and all life. I am happy to say that the ultimate outcome will be the ceasing of all poverty, greed and hatred of others which will mean the end of all wars. From that day forward, love shall truly prevail.

"You and other maverick spearheads are paving the way for a glorious future. This is one reason this work needs to be available to the general public. It will trigger ancient memory codes and help to awaken primordial knowledge that is stored in the very DNA genetic structures of their being. It will help them contact their higher self. In essence, I am your higher self as I am everyone's. Sleepy dreamers are awakening."

"Wake up sleepy dreamers, slumber time is o'er," is the first line of a poem I wrote many years ago," I interrupted.

"Indeed it is."

"Let me think of how it goes. Oh yes, now I remember it.

Wake up Sleepy dreamers! Slumber time is o'er.
We wish to tell you ancient stories that your heart longs to hear once more.

Let them be heard near and far, helping you remember who you are.

You are so much more than what you see.

Extend your vision and glimpse eternity.

Gather in a circle. Hear the Speakers' tales.

Listen very carefully. Listen very well.

Let your mind rest awhile. Listen with your heart.

To the stories the Speakers tell. Sacred whisperings of art.

"That poem, which later became a song, has always haunted me. It stirs up something very ancient."

"Yes it does. It stirs up your ancient archetypal memories of your connection to me. In times long past, you all communicated with me. In time, others will be communicating with me once more just as you and some others are doing now. This makes my heart and soul sing. You are prototypes of the future great men and women who will live in harmony and peace because they have merged the 'male' and 'female' within. As we discussed in the chapter On Love, there can be no harmonious relationships until you have merged with your own logic and intuition, the masculine and feminine components of your self. Once this sacred marriage occurs, then you become truly whole and empowered. At this point, you align with the very forces and energy that underlie creation and you become magic and miracle makers. Michael, you and others are on your way. Learn from those who are ahead of you. They are your mentors, heroes, and heroines. Teach by example those who have not yet come as far as you have. This will help you to advance even more. Give of your light, but do not shine it so brightly that you blind or instill fear. Shine it just enough so that you instill hope. It is hope that ignites the light of their soul."

"Yes," I said, humbly. "The angel who visited me when I was thirteen instilled hope in me. That in turn ignited a light in my soul that never went out no matter how dark my days became. And as you know, I sure had some very dark ones. Boy, you are sure on a roll, Mr. Divine. It's like you are in my head or something. These things you just mentioned I have often thought about,"

Mr. Divine grinned and adjusted his position. "I am known to get in peoples' heads. They need their brains flushed out or a good brainwashing once in awhile. Just call me Mr. Clean."

We both had a good laugh. "I like your sense of humor, Mr. Divine. I invite you to get in my head as often as you wish. Lord knows I still have enough fear, clutter, and baggage in there. Speaking of getting in my head, people have always been able to get in my head. Sometimes it seems I can even read some of their thoughts."

"You can."

"Is it a good feeling to have someone get inside your head?"

"That depends. You do have a lot of activity going on in your head. We will have to look into that some more. Let me say this. You do not have to be psychic to be an energy sender. Some people just do it naturally, often not even realizing what they are doing. Your friend Terry does it a lot to you. He wants what he wants and if it just happens to be your time and energy, he expects you to be there for him."

"Sometimes I mentally tell him to get out of my head. I can feel his anger when he is angry with me. Dad used to get in my head, too. It happened a lot when I was in my first foster home. That almost felt like black magic or something."

"Getting in someone's head does not have to be a negative experience. Can you think of any positive ones?"

"Yes, someone who comes to mind is my friend Chris. I have thought of others kindly and felt their kind thoughts as well. Other times it has felt like people were stalking me psychically. Since I am so sensitive to my surroundings, I even sleep with ear plugs to block out sounds. I also like to keep the bedroom door closed no matter where I am."

"Yes, there can be psychic invasions and intrusions. This is why you shut your computer room door when you work. You do not want any residue energy seeping in. Uplifting music also absorbs negative energy."

"No wonder I always listen to music when I write."

"There is very good energy in your Christmas room. You empower it each time you are there and the energy builds. Negative energy drains you. People who are obsessed with negative emotions such as hatred, anger, bitterness or revenge are especially dangerous to be around; they attract negative entities, who, like attachments, can bombard and psychically attack you."

"I try to keep my energies positive, but sometimes I get zapped. I especially love it when I start drifting off to sleep. I sometimes jokingly say that I am entering sleep's sacred playground. There I see much bigger and grander vistas. Sometimes I can even glimpse the bigger picture of what my life means and is about. At times, ideas and thoughts from my inner knowing come to me out of the blue. My mind feels bigger, my perceptions sharper. It's like I'm in a bigger room in a house."

"In my father's house are many mansions…."

"Sometimes I see shadows dancing, but sometimes they get mean looks on their faces and even call out to me. Sometimes I think Terry's shadow is calling to me. The darkness seems to seek power and energy and it wants more power as its ally so it can become a light absorber. My darkness seeks to devour my own light at times and the light of others, too."

"You have been aware of the power of the darkness for a long time."

"Yes, I think it began with my father and he can still get to me if I let him. Just last month, when we had him home for a visit, he got all bossy with mom and upset her. He always seems to revert to his old dominating controlling self every time we bring him home. In the nursing home, he's a sweet old man. But at home, he takes on that tyrannical tone that makes me want to just smack him. The heaviness of that day simply wore me out. Does it ever end?"

"It ends when you truly will for it to, and sometimes when you are getting close to more breakthroughs and moving more into your light, the darkness comes a calling for a big fight. It does not give up easily."

"How well I know. Just the other day the darkness came a calling. First, Terry sent me some emails which I knew would upset me, so for the first time since I've known him, I deleted them without even reading them. *A little progress*, I thought, *I am not totally flunking.*

"The phone rang a few minutes later and a strange man said, 'I got your name out of the yellow pages. I want to meet with you and target your services to the Hispanic community.' A little while later, another man called saying, 'I have a problem with this girl.' He did not ask for a reading or my rates, or if he could schedule a session. He just wanted instant help on the phone for free. Terry called and was begging to go to Florida with me. I did not pick up the phone. "'No. No. No,' I yelled to the air. 'If I let him go, I'll just come back drained and exhausted. I will have to do all the driving and pay the expenses.' My niece called later and invited me over for dinner. She made foods that I love, but which are not good for my blood pressure. By then, I did not care. I was depressed. I accepted her invitation and pigged out and then felt really awful."

"Do you want peace and calm or do you need the drama of the recent past to give you some excitement?"

"A little excitement makes life interesting, but a little goes a long way as the saying goes."

"It really boils down to do you want to move forward or do you want to go back into the darkness."

I heard a line from something I had written many years ago, "You embraced me last night. I am no longer comforted by your touch. Fear, embrace me no more. I originally put the word 'darkness' embrace me no more, but then the word 'fear' felt more appropriate."

"It is interesting that you use the word fear here. Fear is truly one face of the darkness and to some extent, the words are very related. Shall we hear the writing now?"

"This is another one I have memorized."

"I am all ears, Michael."

Fear, embrace Me No More
You wrapped me in your shroud of black. You held me in your arms many nights. You provided solace for my weary soul.

You caressed my wounded heart. I slept by your side and for a time, I was comforted by your touch. You were a faithful lover. You offered to stay with me until the end of time. You escorted me down many somber streets. You promised me security in your world offering many enticements to tempt me to stay.

But slowly I have begun to see the real you.

You are the prince of oblivion! You rule an unilluminated world. Your fortresses are very high. Darkness is your realm. There are no stars in your sky. Moonless is your night. Black are your eyes. Black are your lips.

Black is your smile. Your soul is obscure. You are not interested in knowing truth because you are the master of death.

It is time for me to go. I have been with you long enough. I must be alone for awhile. I no longer wish to drink from your chalice. There is a need to taste other wine. No time to tarry a moment more. You will not miss me when I depart. There are others who will welcome your kiss.

I do not regret our time together. I look forward to being away from you.

I may fall on my face as I journey alone, but slowly I will find the Light.

You embraced me last night. I am no longer comforted by your touch.

Fear, embrace me no more.

We were quiet a few moments, then I spoke. "The darkness never ceases to come around. Even when I set boundaries, I find that the darkness has no respect and does not honor them."

"In its negative manifestation the darkness seeks only to perpetuate itself and to serve ego. The darkness can be the master of manipulation. You tell it one thing. It listens carefully, then sets about its insidious designs, not giving one thought or care to what you have asked for. For it truly does not care for anything but its selfish designs. It is like a soulless wraith wandering aimlessly until it finds innocent and vulnerable people to feed upon. It has no concept of the meaning of the word boundary, respect or love. The darkness has your image and whereabouts stored in its permanent memory banks. It has instant recall of times when you and others were its ally. We will not get into the past lives where you were its slave. I will just say that the darkness knows about those lives where you were enslaved in its clutches.

"The negative face of your darkness is your hidden fears, your unknowing, your selfishness, the limitations and restrictions you place upon yourself, your addictions and vices and the lack of enlightenment, and love. Fear has been feeding your anger for years and longer – literally many lifetimes. Look at the difficult time your ex-fiancé had getting rid of you, if I might be blunt. You all but stalked her after you two broke up."

"What a sad time of my life. I feel bad about how screwed up and insecure I was then. I know the darkness was manipulating me a lot then."

"You struggled a lot, but you did battle your darkness. Some just give in and allow the darkness to overpower and take control of their lives. You challenged your darkness and reached out for help when you felt yourself sinking deeper into it. You did not want to be controlled by your fears, rage and deep pain. Why do you think you wrote *Fear, embrace Me No More* at that time? It was your soul's way of giving you some insight on what all was going on. You were what some folks in the science fiction field might call a 'halfer'."

"Sounds like a neat idea for a new story or novel."

"Yes, it could be a good one. You were in both worlds- the world of light and the world of night. Actually, everyone is to some degree, but yours was more pronounced because you were more aware of what was transpiring. The difference between you and many other people is that you owned, claimed, and named the darkness. When this happens, its power diminishes and it begins to serve you."

"In some fantasy stories, to reveal your name is to give the opponent access to your power."

"You named the fear or darkness ? The Prince of Oblivion. The ruler of an unilluminated world. The master of death. Terry, and countless others, on the other hand, are still deluded. This is dangerous. They will not name the darkness and be brave enough to see the havoc it is wreaking in their lives. They cannot confront it if they deny it. The darkness has many gifts to offer and most people never come to that realization. They only fear and wish to shun it. Shunning and repressing one's inner darkness never gets rid of it; on the contrary, it magnifies its energy and its power.

"The positive side of the darkness is that it can take you deeper within to discover your own soul faculties and creative resourcefulness. It can show you what is missing in your life and what needs attention. It can show you things that you inwardly know, but outwardly deny about yourself and others. It can bring to the light of day attitudes and beliefs that no longer serve your greater good, but which you hang onto, nonetheless. The darkness can show you when it is time to let go of circumstances, situations and people who are detrimental to your growth. Depression, despair, fear, anger and pain all have their positive sides. They are mighty and powerful teachers. Frustration can push you to move past mediocrity, which enslaves so many people. It can also push you to seek liberation, and yes, growth does come through irritation."

"I think of the old gospel song, 'If I never had a problem, I'd never know that God could solve it,' and a saying – 'every adversity has an equal or greater benefit.'"

"That is true and sadly few people come to believe or realize it. But it is nonetheless true. If your frustrations prod you forward to seek understanding and change, then the darkness has served a positive purpose. The negative side of the darkness is that it can keep you in ignorance, consume and destroy and create misery and death; actually, that is its primary desire and agenda."

"That reminds me of something I read in one of the shaman Carlos Castenada books. His teacher, the great sorcerer, Don Juan, said that death is actually our counselor. It sounds like maybe our darkness could be a similar ally."

"You are getting it now. Death and the Darkness are your mighty counselors. First, you must befriend them, respect them and earn their trust. They will test you severely; you can be sure of that, and often to your very limits. But once you challenge them with all the inner force and strength you can muster, do battle and learn from them, you will discover reservoirs of inner power within you that have been waiting to come to your rescue. Your little *Fear Embrace Me No More* writing is a verbal statement of challenging your darkness. You admit and tell the darkness that you must move on. You must find the light. By acknowledging your darkness, you were granting it respect and honoring and naming it. You did spend time with it. You learned from it and in time, you sought relief from its clutches. You were honest about your dark feelings. You took the journey within to experience your dark nights of the soul.

"You might be amazed at the people whose lives are miserable, but who are so out of touch and in self denial, that they are not even aware of it. It is this awareness and brutal self analysis and honesty that are vital prerequisites to confronting and befriending the darkness. Once this happens, you will begin to feel some sense of relief and your fears, hurts and other negative emotions will also become your allies. Your darkness can teach and guide you and help you understand yourself better. You are wise to give it honor and reverence. Let it become a friend and ally. Most people do everything in their power to avoid and run from their darkness. Many down right deny it. The truth is that there is light and darkness in everyone; it is the way things are on the dualistic realms. There can be neither the one without the other. The goal is to keep them in check and balance. Few do this and they wonder why they are so depressed and unhappy.

"You can transmute much of the negativity of the darkness by merging with it. Your misery and darkness are there to show you what you do not like about yourself and your circumstances. This dislike can motivate you to take measures to change your life. One purpose of the darkness is to get you to moving. If you are just floating on a foggy gray mist, you are doing nothing but sitting on the fence of complacency. You may be smug, but you are not living with the gusto and passion that is your birthright. You are not following your bliss. That is not progress. You do not move forward that way. The essence of the darkness is pure undiluted life force energy. It can propel you to movement and action. The darkness is meant to help you get to the light so you can merge with it.

If you don't believe that you have merged with your darkness, or at least partially, you have but to read any number of your fine writings. They came to you after undergoing many trials and dark nights of the soul. You wrote *Message From My Soul* after an excruciating, dark night of the soul as we talked about early in this book. You have written exquisite love poetry after experiencing pain, rejection and agony in relationships."

"Yeah, to date I have written almost two hundred poems. Sometimes I wonder, why bother?"

"If you will reflect a moment or read some of them, your question will be answered. Your love poems have taken you to the realms of the gods and muses where you have supped and feasted with them at copious sumptuous banquets. Through your art, the muses have revealed sacred mysteries and knowledge. There are jewels and gems spread throughout the verses of your poems. They are personal and universal all in one."

"I recall a line from a poem that said, 'I am a child of the universe. My home is everywhere.'"

"It truly is and yet it is not. The true home is in here," he said, gently tapping me on the heart. Many of your poems point that out and I predict that they will see themselves in print. They will deeply move and inspire many people. Yes, I can see how baffling it can be to be told that it is your sorrow that has led you to the heights of bliss and ecstasy that you explore in many of your transcendental poems."

"Or as Gibran says in The Prophet, 'the deeper that sorrow carves into your being, the more joy you can contain,' I added."

"Touché, Michael! Your despair resonated so loudly that Heaven's gates opened and sent you an angelic visitation when you were thirteen. Your loneliness was so potent that even I heard its plaintive lament. Your plea for help was so sincere and desperate that I had no choice but to come to you. There is great power in despair, agony and surrender. This is what people must come to know so they can come to embrace their despair instead of running from or trying to eradicate it. I know this is not easy to digest and assimilate and many never do. But for those who do, Heaven opens to receive them and they are sent all the help they need. And they become victorious!"

"I know. I believe you, Mr. Divine. It's just so hard to take this all in. Gibran says 'for even as love crowns you, so shall he crucify you.' I feel that I have been crucified."

"You have, and like beloved Jesus, you have come back alive more radiant and powerful than before. Everyone must be crucified, or metaphorically speaking, the ego must die and be reborn."

"Yes, as St. Francis of Assisi says in his prayer of peace, 'It is in dying that we are born to eternal life.'"

"The truth was never better spoken."

"Whoa, this is a lot to take in. I need a drink."

"Yes, Michael this is taking things to a much deeper level of awareness and experience, but I thought it might be the time to bring this up to you. When you merge with the darkness, you accept its reality in your life. You accept that its negative and positive traits are always going to be there. Which pole you express is always up to you. A true master can bring light into any field of darkness and transmute it so that both the light and the darkness are changed. This brings about a state of equanimity. When this is achieved, there is balance and harmony. You are then said to be 'in your power or empowered'. At this level of attainment, you are not affected by the woes and negativity of the world; neither the negativity inside or outside of you. You are working diligently to arrive at this deeper and more enlightened understanding. Note that the two words deeper and enlightened are almost interchangeable here.

"One of the reasons you went back home and lived with your mother was to work more with this realization. One of the indications that there is more balancing to be achieved is when you find yourself using the word 'never'. Never say never has become real popular in the new thought movement and rightly so. Another way to say the same thing is, 'That which you resist, persists.' Since you talked about your new home becoming a sanctuary for you earlier, I thought I would bring it up that you have proven that you can go back home. For years, you swore you would never ever, not on your deathbed, move back home."

"That is right. There were too many memories of terrible things that took place in that house. I remember how I used to wish the house would just burn down. I felt that might somehow erase some of the bad memories."

"It might on the surface level, but that is all. The true erasing and healing of bad memories must take place within you. It is a journey that you and everyone can only make alone. When that happens, it does not matter what outer signs you have to remind you of the past. Going back home can be done, but I am not saying it is easy."

"You can say that again. It took me months to begin to feel comfortable there. I would not even watch a movie for months. When I first moved in with mom, I was not there for more than a night or two at a time. I'd always find an excuse to not be there. I often visited my sister and there was my work which gave me the opportunity for travel."

"Michael, you never forgot your deeper intention to heal your self to the point that even your memories no longer hurt or haunted you."

"I guess I did keep plugging away. Little by little, I made the place my own. I planted flowers, repainted my brother's room, and several rooms in the colors my mother wanted. In time, I found myself able to sit on the porch at night enjoying the breeze and the evening sunset. In time, my sleep became more restful and I found that sad memories of those long ago yesterdays stopped visiting me so much. Now, they seldom do. I am still shocked and surprised that I came back home to live. I had sworn never to do that."

"Perhaps you will never say never again."

"Yes, although at times, I also know we have to keep away from the physical proximity of certain people or places to protect our selves from old hurts, pain, and anger."

"There is a place for staying away and you stayed away from your childhood home most of your adult life. You also knew deep inside that you wanted to be able to come back home and not be affected adversely. You wanted to overcome and conquer the mass feelings of depression that would overwhelm you when you came home. And yes, timing is crucial in the healing process."

"I remember spending one night there many years ago. I slept on the couch and had nightmares all night. It was horrible. I never spent the night again for years. It was worse when Dad was still there, but not over when he went to the nursing home. You are right. It has been a real challenge to come to grips with that house and to be able to stay there."

"In that sense, you and the darkness in this house have merged and created a new energy. In a sense, you now like the house and it likes you. It even feels like a home. You have given it some of your new understandings and it has taken them in. Thus its own energy and mood have changed as yours have. You have succeeded at moving a lot of residual energy that was stored in your house. Painting and renovating can help, but only if you have done the internal renovating and work as well. Because you have never lost sight of your goal to heal, the house has been receptive and helpful to you in that endeavor. The house has even helped heal your inner child in some ways and is still doing so as you have helped heal the house and some of the memories therein.

"You can go home again! You are feeling better about yourself. Many of the fears that have held you back are fading. You are getting braver and are charging ahead with your new dreams. Now you want to see other places. Other homes. Other states. The travel bug and the wanderlust are grabbing you more, are they not?"

"In the past year, I have been to Florida twice, to Mammoth Cave four times, To Gatlinburg, Tennessee, King's Island and taken some other shorter journeys."

"There will be many more. As strange as it may seem, your childhood house is alive. Of course, not in the way that plants, animals or humans are, but alive nonetheless. Inanimate objects draw upon the energy of those possessing and touching them.

Thought forms, emotions of love, anger, joy and pain all get stored within the very walls of houses and buildings. Some houses are said to be very angry. Some are very loving. Some are haunted."

"That sounds like something from the Amityville horror movies."

"I have told you before that there is truth couched in your fiction tales if you look for it. We will go into this in more detail in the chapter 'Fantasy possesses elements of truth.' You wrote a very interesting little scene in your novel not long ago about this very subject."

I lit up. "Oh, yes, it was the one where my character Cindy asked the strange man how he got into the house and he responded that the house invited him inside. That scene just popped right in my head like all the others do."

"For your information, your novel is not totally fiction even though I know you probably would never sell it as anything but fiction."

"I fear I may never sell this book if I don't call it fiction. People are going to think I'm nuts to dare make a claim that you are talking to me, even if I only say it's in dreams."

"Be positive. The public is warming up more and becoming less skeptical about such possibilities. You say these are dream conversations. Does it matter? Not to me. The important thing is to get the word out there that I am alive and well and very interested in having a personal relationship with each and every one. What is important is the information that comes through, not its format. We have been through this before."

"I know and I believe you in my heart. I just have my doubts sometimes."

"That is part of being human and hopefully in time, they will decrease. Now, back to houses being alive. Your childhood house has helped free you to some extent. Now that you feel safe there, you can feel safe at other places."

"I can just see the sneers I'd get if I told this to most people."

"Let them sneer. What do they know? Since most of them are not as sensitive or as creative as you, I might add, they know little about the subtle influences of energy and the power of places where strong emotional ties and attachments exist. You felt imprisoned for so many years, and it never occurred to you that the very place you feared imprisoned you, was actually the one place that was able to help heal your painful past. Again, your darkness held the key to open the door to the light."

"You are right. This all sounds very strange, but it resonates."

"Just review your basic quantum physics when you need confirmation. All matter moves at the quantum levels. There you have energy and molecule movements. Inanimate objects can take on more of the energy of the holders whereas plants, trees and flowers have more independent life force. You have read the studies that say that plants respond to music. They also respond to love and kindness. People with the proverbial "green thumbs" know this. Take yourself, for example. For years you had nothing to do with plants and flowers. Over the years, as you became more sensitive and loving to yourself and others, you became more attracted to plants and flowers."

"I can't imagine not having lots of plants and flowers around me now. It is a joy to spend some quiet time in the evenings outside enjoying all my beautiful flowers. I talk to them and look at them and give gratitude for their beauty. I take note of every new blossom and enjoy watching them grow and watering them. I get so distressed when I see yards where people do not tend to their plants. I have even been known to sneak water to a few who were wilting and drying out. Flowers are so beautiful. How can people not make time for them and give them the proper care they deserve?"

"People get too busy and caught up in their own drama and lives."

"Well, I sure have done that and had my own share of drama to say the least. But one thing is for certain, when I had no interest in plants and flowers, I simply didn't buy any."

"Now you are the 'flower king,'" Mr. Divine said with a grin on his face. People comment on how lovely your flowers are and the exquisite aroma of your roses. They do respond to all the love and attention you give them."

"I have been really pleased with that big peace lily plant my brother gave me after Dad's funeral. It grows new leaves all the time. I talk to that plant everyday. Last week I spotted a white bloom beginning. I got so excited and can hardly wait for it to fully blossom. Then there is the poinsettia plant I have had since before last Christmas. A few weeks ago it was down to one red leaf and two green ones. I did not have the heart to toss it out. I kid you not, a few days later the plant was down to one leaf. I was about to take it outside for the compost pile, but instead I found myself looking at it. 'I like you,' I spontaneously said, 'you can't die on me. I really enjoy having you around.' Then I went out of town for a week. When I returned, ten new leaves were sprouting. Do you think the plant understood me? Do I sound nuts?"

"Absolutely not."

"I was so astounded and surprised. Did the plant feel my love and sense my energy? More leaves began to sprout. And now some six weeks later that poinsettia plant is making a major comeback. From the two remaining stems, some twenty two leaves have sprouted. That is my miracle plant! I did not want it to die. I asked the plant to live and that is what it did. Is this nuts?"

"Absolutely not. The plant feels your love and energy and is responding. Enjoy it. Talk to it. Many people talk to plants. Plants perceive the energy that is projected to and around them and they respond in their own subtle ways."

"I know this kind of talking sounds nuts, but yet I know it is not. I have my poinsettia plant to prove what you are saying."

"Everyone should have flowers to enjoy. They are the perfect symbol of beauty and a grand metaphor for the blossoming of the soul. On that note, I shall take my leave. You look like you could use some more rest."

"Thanks for visiting."

Chapter Fifteen

The Voice Behind Your Voice

"I am the voice behind your voice," were the first words my divine guest spoke to me a few days later.

"That is one of my writings," I said softly.

"Yes," Mr. Divine replied. "You wrote it after a dream about art and beauty."

"Yes, I recall. I wrote a little preface which said, 'art and beauty connect you to the divine. Beauty and art connect you to the "one," the source from which you came. They give you a glimpse of your true self. The sooner you discard the mask of the false self that you wear, the more clearly the true self can manifest through you.' I remember that day vividly. I didn't want to come out of the dream. I wanted to go back to that place of beauty."

"Michael, you were tapping celestial realms in your dreams long ago. It happens to many people and far more than you think."

"Thank goodness. My life was in one mess back then."

"I know and there is no harm in taking nocturnal repose in dream time. It is a nice way to recharge your spiritual batteries, so to speak. Those places are real and you can visit them anytime you wish. Your life was in such turmoil and upheaval back then. You needed to glimpse a larger perspective, your larger perspective. You may not recall, but before you fell asleep the night of that dream, you prayed, 'Dear God, there has to be more than this, there just has to be. Please let there be more so I can get through this.'"

"I'm not surprised. In my desperation, I'm sure I uttered a lot of similar prayers."

"Prayer is powerful, especially when it is offered with faith and gratitude for it being answered. Said another way, the call does compel the response."

I looked out into the distance, my eyes taking on that faraway look I sometimes get. "There is more, isn't there?"

"Yes, there is and when you said, 'Dear God, there has to be more than this,' you were exercising the faith required to bring 'more' to you. You knew in your heart even though you were in pain and your ego had its doubts. Everyone knows there is more. Their soul knows. It is the soul that we address, for the truth always resonates to the soul. You believed in your soul that I was real and could come to you. That knowing made it so. Now that I am here, let me reiterate that I am always here for you. I am always here for you and for everyone. You have but to still your restless mind by going within the silence; it is there where I meet you."

"I know, but still I sometimes I feel so alone. When I'm in the pit, it's like nothing but the darkness exists. Nothing seems to help or give relief during those times."

"Sometimes you choose to experience different nuances of the darkness so you can better see and know the light, but one thing is for certain – when you have had enough and you truly call out from the soul, help is always forthcoming."

"The call compels the response."

"Always. It can be no other way."

"I know this, but sometimes I just plain forget. When I'm in that dark pit, it's like out of sight, out of mind. Nothing else seems to exist or matter."

"When you can do nothing else but weep and curl up in a corner, know that you can do one thing. Call out to me and try your best to believe that I am there."

"I have done that, haven't I?"

"Many times, and you did so the night of your dream when this writing came to you."

"I remember feeling sorry for myself, thinking that no one would ever love me and that I was doomed to be alone forever." Then I said, more softly, "I remember wanting to die."

"Do you remember wanting to stop the voices inside your head that were telling you terrible things?"

"Yes. They can be ruthless."

"At one point, you said, 'Please, God, shut up these voices. Sometimes I wish I had no voice at all. The words I speak are bitter. The words I hear in my mind are worse. Isn't there a voice behind my voice that can speak of better things?' You fell asleep whispering, "Where is the voice behind the voice?""

"Are you the voice behind my voice?"

"Listen to what you wrote that morning and then you tell me."

"Yes, it is another of my favorites," I replied, then began reciting.

The Voice Behind Your Voice

I am the voice behind your voice. I inspire poets, musicians, and artisans. I whisper my messages softly to all. Some hear me. Others do not. Yet my whispers haunt those who listen not. I am the universal sound from which all languages are derived. I spoke to you all before you learned to speak. Before the creation of words and alphabets. If you will close your eyes and open your heart, you will hear me. Remember, there are those who do. I give them verses.

Those of you afraid to enter the souls' secret chamber say, "He is a gifted poet. He is different from me." But occasionally even you must stop. You admire a sunset and you say, "Tis painted by the hand of God."

For a few moments, you stand still. You are wordless. Why? Because you are listening to me speak through beauty. "Who am I?" I have told you once. I will tell you again. You can hear a little better this time. Why do you think I give you sunsets, roses, or stars in the sky? To remind you for a moment of that part of yourself that lives and never dies. Who are you? You ask again. I am the voice behind your voice. You will be Love when all illusions are gone. To be one with me requires great work. It is the life purpose of every woman and man. Just listen. Go within and hear my voice behind your voice again and again!"

Tears were dripping down my face. I was in such awe to be in his presence even though he had told me many times that a beautiful spark shines inside my own soul and inside the soul of everyone else. I wanted to speak, but could not.

A few minutes later Mr. Divine spoke gently.

"I am with you from the beginning and unto the end of this world and worlds upon end."

"During that moment I believed him with all my heart and soul.

Chapter Sixteen

On Sadness

I was on a high for days after that last visit with Mr. Divine. I seemed to feel his presence everywhere. He didn't visit for several days, but it was as though I could hear his voice in everything. I dreamed that night that I was lying in a big hammock. All was quiet and peaceful. An angel appeared overhead and whispered, "Let yourself be embraced by eternity's sweet kiss!" I woke up whispering "eternity's sweet kiss." I wanted to write a song about it. It occurred to me that if God were love and everything else, then every sound was some divine uttering. Maybe that is the voice behind the voice that he spoke of. He/She/It must be "the self" behind all of our selves.

Mr. Divine showed up promptly the next morning. After some chitchat over coffee, he asked me what I wanted to talk about today.

"Sadness. I have struggled with feelings of despair and sadness all of my life. What can you tell me about sadness?"

"Sadness is one of those emotions that grips people far too often. "That so saddens me, for when you are sad, then so am I. Let us speak on sadness more in depth now, Michael. Actually this topic came up some years ago when you were thinking about sadness. The result was an essay that you wrote called *On Sadness*. Why don't you share that with your readers?"

"It's funny how I always wanted to be an actor. I could never memorize scripts very well, but memorizing my own writings seems to come naturally."

"That is because matters of human drama are not a priority to you; it is matters of the soul that are to take precedence. Now, before we hear *On Sadness,* please tell us what was going on in your life when you wrote it.

"It was one of those days when my mind was restless. To help alleviate the boredom and anxiety I was feeling, I took a walk. I must have been gone four or five hours. I seemed to lose myself in people watching. One thing I noticed was that so many people's faces had this sad look. The sun was shining bright and beautifully. We were in full Spring with lush flowers blooming everywhere; the lovely scents and fragrances were intoxicating. The cool breeze was rejuvenating Yet, why did so many people look so sad? Because they are, I remembered telling myself. My mind took a journey down memory lane and I relived many of my own sad times. I even named one of my inner characters 'sad Little Michael'.   It was not long before my sunny mood disappeared, and I, like the others, took on that empty sorrowful look.

"When I got home, I kept thinking that we are just not meant to live that way. Sure, it is natural to be sad from time to time, but to take on that perpetual look of sadness is not normal. I meditated in my big comfy chair and fell asleep. When I woke up a half hour later, I had the urge to write. The words just flowed.

Mr. Divine grinned and with a twinkle in his eyes let me know that something was up. I wanted to ask if he inspired the "writing" but I refrained.   He smiled again, then I recited *On Sadness*.

On Sadness

"Drinking from the cup of sadness is a commonly practiced ritual by people who identify with the human self. Celestial beings and those cognizant of their divinity, live in harmony with all creation.   For them, there are no false perceptions or separation from the life force which permeates every one and every thing. Identifying with their macrocosmic self allows them to live peaceful lives. However, the majority of people overly identify with the microcosmic ego self, which has little understanding of the interconnection of matter and spirit.

"A fundamental understanding of this interconnection offers a sense of oneness and kinship to all. Dissolving the erroneous limiting perceptions that others are inherently different, awakens one to a natural trust and respect for people and all life. Trust and respect open the door to the true essence of the self, which is love.

"Love knows no sense of separation, guilt, or pain. When the true essence (love) of life flows through one's being, the mind cannot fool the self to believe it can be hurt. Only the personality can perceive pain, lack, and the absence of unity. The personality or ego experiences sadness when it forgets its connection to the self. Believing itself to be incomplete and in need of others to feel a sense of wholeness, it becomes attached to various persons, desiring and expecting them to fill the void of emptiness in their soul. The ego truly believes that another person can offer happiness and joy. In reality, joy and happiness are not qualities of the self, but of the personality. Sadness and all sentiments are created by the personality through the emotional body which was formed by the human ego. Transient emotions come and go like the changing seasons. To place one's trust in and to surrender to ephemeral sentiments is an open invitation to drink from the cup of sadness and sorrow.

"We do not discourage people from tasting from this cup, but rather remind them that the sweetness of joy or the bitterness of sorrow do not last. Taste from this cup with the understanding that to experience emotional reactions is a temporary inebriation. At first, the "self" played with emotional reactions in total non-identification, never forgetting its oneness with the Great All That Is that some refer to as God. Slowly, its constant amusement and attention to its self-centered ego, led it to identify with its creation until finally it totally forgot its connection to the source.

"Sadness can only be experienced by sleeping mortals unaware of their 'great self', which is the essence of all life. The ego, or little self, in its self-centered thinking, depends on the ego of others for sense gratification, emotional nurturing, and physical attention and excitement. Self deception causes it to believe others can offer magical bliss through the experience people call 'falling in love.' This expression is partially true in the sense that believing oneself to be in love does involve a fall; the fall from awareness of inherent wholeness.   The fall from the total awareness of 'the self' gave birth to pain and sadness.

"We do not discourage communing and sharing with others. The desire to share is a natural inclination of the self. Sharing expands creativity and awareness. It fills the mind, heart and soul with loving thoughts and energy and enhances intimacy. There are infinite varieties and ways for people to share on your Earth and on endless other worlds. We simply encourage mortals to remember not to attempt to direct another's actions to serve one's own ego centered motives.

Free yourselves from your ego's expectations of others, allowing spontaneous sharing to occur. Surrender to your own soul, allowing your own Great Self, the I am that I am, to direct your thoughts and destiny. Then peace will begin to flow through your being. At this time, sadness will fade like tracks on the sand being effaced by the ocean's waves. Remember these words and be at peace!"

I slowly opened my eyes. I took several minutes to absorb the words I had just heard. Although I knew the words had come from or through me, they still did not feel like words I would write. They must have originated from another source. I wanted to ask my divine guest if he was the one who inspired the "writing," but the look on his face left me speechless and filled my very soul with joy. Somehow I knew he had a hand in my writing and that filled me with great comfort.

I closed my eyes again and asked Mr. Divine who the 'we' speaking in the writing was. He smiled and gently touched my hand then spoke softly.

"We are one and we are many. We are the 'one' with many names and the one with no names. We are the ascended light beings. We are the collective hidden 'self' of humanity. We are I and I are we and we love you. Know this and be sad no more."

I slowly opened my tear-filled eyes. I wanted to say thank you but my divine guest had disappeared. And yet somehow I felt his presence. Peace enfolded my entire being. After so much sadness and turmoil in the past this serenity was a most welcomed guest.

Chapter Seventeen

On Mourning

I had an interesting dream the following night. I was sitting underneath a huge weeping willow tree. Weeping willows are my favorite trees, so I'm not surprised that I found myself beneath one. A fairy dressed in a light blue flowing gown sat next to me and said, "You get sad because you feel that something is missing in your life. That something, is none other than 'you' she continued, tapping my heart gently. "You miss your self and this makes you sad. Some day you are going to step through time and rendezvous with every you who has ever been, or ever will be. Then you will not feel sad. You are going to learn that none of the 'yous' have ever died. Not only the yous of You, but the 'yous' of others as well; those people dear to your heart. Death is not unkind as people credit him to be. He is the deliverer who escorts the soul back to its natural home – the dwelling abode of spirit. He is also known in our circles as the 'good friend'."

"I wrote something like that once. 'The moment you are born, a part of you dies. When you die again, you shall be born.'"

"You got it," she said, snickering. "When you learn this, then you will cease to have the need for mourning. 'Your mourning days are nigh over,'" she whispered several times. Then she stood up, made a curtsy, blew me a kiss, and was gone.

When I woke up, I could still see the blue fairy's form, so light, so playful and ethereal. I wanted to go where she went. "She has gone to the playground of gladness" I heard. Then Mr. Divine appeared.

"Good morning, Michael. You have many playmates on other dimensions and Elorielle is one of them. You sometimes visit her in dream time. It is time for you to acquire some further understanding on mourning which is similar to sadness. Like Elorielle said, your mourning days are nigh over."

"I hope so because I am still mourning the death of my younger brother who died back in 1997. Though part of me knows he is still alive and well, I still mourn him."

"You are in good company. Well, a little essay you wrote back at the time you wrote sadness may give you some insight and consolation."

I lit up. "I did write an essay called *On Mourning*, didn't I?" I haven't thought of that one in a long time."

"Shall we hear it now?"

"Oh, yes please."

I took a couple of deep breaths then began.

On Mourning

It is the false belief that life unkindly snatches dear ones away that leads mortals to experience mourning. Many perceive that when Life calls her children to walk through the portal of death, that she eradicates their personality, effacing their spirit into nothingness. How could Life be so unkind as to desire to separate you from those souls dear to your hearts? She would never attempt such a cruel act. When the self surrenders its human form to return to dust, the essence of life is not temporarily suspended or terminated.

The "self" has always lived and always will. A lifetime is but a moment in eternity, a speck of sand on a beach ever moving to the dance of the ocean's waves. It does not resist its destiny. Likewise, the "self" moves through one form to another in order to express itself through material energy much the same way as one may wear a variety of garments on different occasions. The "self" creates human emotions and desires and then often forgets its divine origin, choosing to identify with its creations. For a time, it slumbers in the terrestrial fields of human illusion. Yet its vision is never completely clouded, and forgetfulness fades when the dawn of remembrance approaches.

Slowly, the "self" remembers its divine origin, realizing that all people are living souls manipulating human form as a puppeteer playfully maneuvers the strings of the marionette. When the "self" has satisfied the desire for diversion, it lays the body down as the puppeteer lays down the marionette. When the "self" realizes that it possesses a body, but is not the body, then the belief in loss and separation fades. In its stead will dawn the realization that the person, whose body has returned to the earth whence it came, has not died. Physical separation need not sever your ties to your loved ones.

Think of them with fervent love and deep concentration. Visualize their form. Recall fond memories. If you persist, you will feel their presence. Your thoughts are powerful invisible energy spirals which can be directed to anyone anywhere and attract those people you refer to as the departed. They have departed from your physical presence, but it is their personality and spirit you so dearly love and cherish. Therefore, when you think about the departed, you are sending out an etheric message to their spirit or essence which survives physical dissolution. Few people receive this contact because their restless chaotic thoughts block the higher mental faculties which transcend time and space.

If you still your mind in daily quiet and meditation, your sensitivity will heighten. With persistence, you can contact anyone who practices this discipline be they on this plane or others. Those beyond your third dimension are usually more receptive to your thoughts because they have access to higher intuitive perceptions that most people do not develop on the Earth. This does not invalidate their existence. All can enjoy contact with those dear to them. As a letter from a friend can warm the heart without the person's physical presence, likewise can a departed loved one or intuitive person send you thoughts. When you utilize your deeper cognitive faculties, mourning will become obsolete in your experience.

In reality, all dimensions exist simultaneously. Your genius' have but tapped the surface of the tip of the iceberg of everyone's inherent divinity and creative potential. Identify less with the mortal self, and more with your divine self. There is no task a focused will cannot accomplish. Believe in yourselves. Those you love can never die. They are alive whether on the Earth or in spirit realms.

Why do we speak this with confidence? Because the essence of the Self is Love and Love never dies. Be joyous and mourn no more!

Hearing that did give me consolation. I knew I would always miss my baby brother, but perhaps now my heart pain might diminish as I realized that he is alive and well and receptive to my thoughts and energy. It gave me some comfort to think that I could meet him on a different plane, the soul spirit plane. There, we could have visits and get to know one another in ways that were not possible during his short life here on the Earth.

I thanked Mr. Divine, then he said, "The veils that separate you from your loved ones are but mere shadowy wisps, mere illusion. You can now have the brotherly relationship that you and Bradley missed out on. Never forget this, Michael." Then he gave a little bow, "I'll be on my way now."

I woke up thinking about Bradley. I somehow felt his presence and that warmed my heart.

Chapter Eighteen

On Hatred

A couple days later, I reread *On Sadness* and *On Mourning* after I had my morning coffee. The doubting Thomas part of me lit into me, telling me that I just made it all up to soothe my own loneliness and to offer some explanations for my own unknowing.

"What do you really know about the workings and the forces of destiny beyond your tiny third dimensional experience and small field of awareness?" this part of me asked. "What makes you think there is a 'greater picture' to yours or anyone's life, or any greater meaning to life other than what you can see and experience directly? How arrogant of you to think you can figure anything out!"

The questions went on and I honored them. I had learned long ago to welcome the many "mes" at the dinner table, metaphorically speaking. My therapist, Elizabeth, had taught me to do that, and I had found it very beneficial. I could always challenge the different parts of me (sub-personalities) just as I always loved to challenge my Philosophy and Religion professors in college.

The doubting Thomas part of me continued his rampage for awhile. I did not respond. I simply remained open to the possibility that he could very well be right and that he could equally be wrong. That seemed fair enough to me. I thought about discussing my latest Doubting Thomas experience with Mr. Divine the next time he paid me a visit. I reread the writings and was grateful to have them. They gave me food for thought, and I found the implications in them interesting, exciting and mind boggling at times. So instead of trying to figure things out, I decided I'd just go with the writings when they came and absorb what I could from them over time.

I still felt on a roll and wanted to write about something else. What to write about next? Several ideas popped in my head, but Mr. Divine showed up the next morning with two steamy cups of freshly brewed Hazelnut coffee. We sat at my kitchen table and chatted a few minutes, then he took on a serious look and said. "Why not write about hatred?"

"Hatred, I'm not sure I'm ready for that."

"Sure you are, it is a subject you have been interested in and have a lot of experience with. Let's talk about that some now. I am all ears."

Mr. Divine was right about my interest in the subject matter. It had taken years to admit that I had hatred for my father. The subject had come up in my early days of therapy with Elizabeth. When she first proposed that my inner child, little Michael, as she referred to him, had hatred for his father, I denied it adamantly. "No, way," I said, "I have worked through that hatred. I wish my father well now and feel only love for him. I have totally forgiven him."

"Maybe the adult Michael has forgiven your father," Elizabeth challenged, "but little inner child Michael could give one hoot about what the adult you claims. I am telling you that part of little Michael hates his father, and rightly so. He never had a chance to express his pain and anger for all the mean horrible things his father did. He had to shove all those feelings and that anger down until it brewed to the point that it turned into rage. Look at the rage and anger you have been carrying around for years. I tell you, and I think I can venture to say confidently so, that some of that rage is directed to your father. The only way you are going to get to the love and release the hatred, is to admit and confront it. You have got to let little Michael feel it and let him pour out all that pain he has been carrying inside for years. He also needs to grieve his lost childhood and perhaps you need to grieve some of your past lives as well."

"That impressed me. Elizabeth was my first therapist to openly admit her belief in reincarnation. That was the icing on the cake in addition to her being an excellent psychotherapist. I had told her about some of my traumatic lives I had learned about in some past life regressions and readings. She listened attentively and said she agreed that some of my rage and hurt could stem from other lifetimes. But she was also adamant that much of it stemmed from this lifetime as well and needed to be confronted and dealt with before I could release the rage and deep inner pain.

"I agreed; the proof being all of the years I was unhappy. I had been struggling with depression for years. I had a short temper at times and could be very impatient and even selfish. I knew about my rage and often felt like a bomb ready to explode any moment. She was right. It was time to get at the root of some things. I decided it was time for change and thus began yet another intense "round" as I refer to it, of my inner child healing work. I had done some years ago in college with therapists and from reading Psychology Self Help books. Although I had made progress, I still had a long way to go. In college, my intellect was very active. I could analyze and discuss the concepts I read about to the point that some therapists said I knew more than they did. But I did not do well when it came to "the feeling" part.

"Elizabeth and I did gestalt therapy exercises and active imagination scenarios where I confronted my father about the terrible things he did. There were many moments of tears, screaming at other times, and the reliving of many painful memories. It would take a book or two to record those sessions and all they did for me.

"Yes, I had come to realize the only way I could learn to forgive and love my father was to deal with the part of me that hated him. I can still recall that session where we relived the time when my father pulled a knife on my sister and threatened to kill her. After she had testified against him in court for raping her, he had broken the restraining order and sneaked home one day. He took out a pocket knife and was rubbing it back and forth. We were in the bedroom changing baby Bradley after a bath when dad sneaked in the house. He told my sister that if any father had the right to kill his daughter, it was him. My mother, probably the only time in her life, intervened, and we somehow managed to get away and call the police. "Elizabeth had me do an imaginary exercise where little Michael visits a wizard who gave him the ability to become anyone he wanted. He could be Superman, Spiderman, The Hulk, whoever. I chose to be the Hulk. I remember seeing myself grow into a giant mass of bulging muscles. In my imagination, I was "The Hulk."

"Elizabeth then asked me, as little Michael, what I wanted to do with my father. "You can beat him up if you wish; you can kill him if you want. You can do whatever you wish. You are The Hulk and your father is at your mercy."

"I will never forget the little childlike voice that came out of me speaking softly, "I don't want to hurt daddy. I just want him to stop hurting my Mommy." That broke my heart. Just asking little Michael how he felt and what he wanted did so much for my healing. I had feared for years that part of me would actually want to kill my father, and when I gave little Michael the opportunity in a therapy fantasy exercise, to my surprise, I discovered that what he really wanted was quite different. That and other exercises helped clear up some hatred; I knew that I was beginning to heal."

Tears dripped down my face as I recalled those long ago times. "Yes, I had known great hatred and learned much from it. I am convinced that it is my learning to admit and deal with my hatred that kept me from going over the edge. There is something very healing about letting ourselves experience and relive our emotions that have been pent up for so long. Holding them in eats away at us and steals our joy, passion for life and drains our energy. It can even lead to health problems or cancer. It certainly kept me in a constant state of depression. By doing some whooping and hollering, some crying and some screaming, I was able to transmute and move energy that had been blocking and keeping me locked into my own prison of hatred for years.

"We are often not aware of the need to grieve or we may convince ourselves we have done so, when we either have not, or we have only partially grieved that which we have lost or been deprived of. As we worked more and more, I found myself fully diving in. I relived the lonely, scary nights at home when I'd pray to be asleep when Dad got home so I would not have to hear the fights. I relived the loneliness of not being able to have friends spend the night because I never knew when some trifle might set Dad off. I relived the sadness I felt when I was five years old at Dad being gone all day at work and even when he was home he paid little attention to me. I relived not getting a bicycle when my brothers and sister got one. I relived Dad not attending the high school musical I had a part in, nor my graduation ceremony just because he was in one of his usual bad moods. I relived my second grade teacher taking me to the clothing room when I was seven and going home with a big brown paper bag full of shirts, socks, sweaters and pants. In my child innocence, when the kids made fun of me one day in the gym for having holes in my socks, I told my teacher the truth. I didn't have any socks without holes in them. 'We can fix that,' she had said and took me to the clothing room where students and parents would donate clothing for the needy. My father threw a fit and spanked me, insisting that no child of his accepted charity and made me take the clothes back. I wanted to tell my teacher that he had money for booze, but none to buy me new socks. I relived other sad memories."

Then I became self conscious, realizing how long I had been talking. I looked up at Mr. Divine. His eyes radiated their usual glow, but I sensed sadness in them too. "You surely don't wish to hear of such things," I said, feeling embarrassed. "I have gone on long enough. Shouldn't we be talking of more celestial matters?"

"Healing the heart and the emotions is a celestial matter," he corrected me. "You cannot take your material possessions with you when you go, as the saying goes, but you take any unhealed parts of yourself with you. The unresolved hurts and conflicts that get repressed and dumped into the subconscious mind do not disappear. They will have to be dealt with and confronted in a future lifetime on the Earth. I am very glad to listen to your stories and I encourage everyone to tell their own stories. There is great healing and comfort that results when you tell your stories. Now, I want you to read that essay *On Hatred* you wrote some years ago. I want you to savor it. I will take my leave now so you can do just that."

I woke up a few minutes later and took out my pen and notebook from my nightstand drawer and rapidly took down notes. It was as though the dream conversations were somehow placed in my mind. Once I started writing, the words just flowed effortlessly. No matter how many dream visits I had with Mr. Divine, I was still mystified at my ability to recall the conversations near verbatim. A few minutes later, I pulled out my little booklet of essays. I closed my eyes and acknowledged my soul, Mr. Divine, my guides and angels, thanking them for always being there for me and helping me with all my trials. I mentally thanked the social workers, and therapists, especially Elizabeth, for their encouragement and belief in my ability to heal and for their patience. I thanked my muse for the many gifts, poems, stories and writings. This all fuels my determination to continue the battle no matter how low or depressed I might become.

I only have to recall those horrible childhood memories and I know that miracles and magic exist. Angels watch over us all. We are never alone and "the call does compel the response." Help came to me and it can come to anyone who asks for it. But we have to ask. God, the angels, and our own soul will not force themselves upon us. This I have learned. With these thoughts in mind, I took a few deep breaths and tried to clear my mind. "Come to me, Oh, my soul," I said. "It is time for me to hear some thoughts on hatred that I might better understand this most potent emotion. I took out the booklet and turned to *On Hatred*.

On Hatred

Hatred results from the faulty perception that someone outside yourself possesses the key to your happiness and fulfillment. Those who feel incomplete look to another to fill the void inside their heart. Such attempts invariably lead to frustration and further emptiness because incompletion is not an inherent characteristic of the soul. To believe otherwise is to misperceive one's true essence. The belief of incompletion of the soul is only born in the mind who has descended to the illusory mode of dualistic thinking.

Hatred can only be experienced when you believe that your peace and joy depend upon the actions of another, and when this other withholds attention, or what may be perceived as love, frustration ensues, leading to anger which can lead to feelings of hatred. Only those alienated from their true nature are capable of perceiving hatred for another human being. Fiery emotional outbursts are the result of clinging efforts to direct either one's own or another's destiny. Some do believe they can exert their will upon another for selfish ego gratification. Hatred results when the imposer's designs are thwarted through the resistance of another's will.

If everyone surrendered all desire to control or impose upon another, then hatred would melt as a snowflake, and the soul could pour forth such love from within for which all mortals search and hunger. To hate another is an external projection of deep inner turmoil and self loathing. Such troubled ones believe themselves to be split and search diligently for that perfect person with whom to unite. When the person does not live up to their ideal expectations, they search once more seeking another whose heart they would seek to possess under the guise of love. In reality, such deluded ones are attempting to capture love who always flees from those who would cling. You cannot grasp love for even a moment. If you are worthy, love may approach you, but she flees from all who attempt to capture her.

Examine your concept of hatred and see if an inner voice will not reveal the fallacy that to depend upon another for love is to deny your own divine nature and essence. Recognize love in yourself, then you will see it in others. The heart that awakens to this truth will then be filled with boundless love for all life. When you are embraced by the supreme truth, you will never again feel alone or separated. Everyone awaits this divine embrace. Know that the rays of deeper understanding will illuminate your consciousness, effacing ignorance and attachments. Illumination dissipates the mist of hatred and anger.

Look within and discover that you are whole and complete. The creative infinite intelligence endowed every one with an independent will and ability to discover that there are no secrets or mysteries to penetrate. Knowledge, wisdom, and happiness are contained within the chamber of the heart. No one need search another's heart for the missing key. There is no need. The chamber was never locked. Everyone has access to this chamber where nothing is lacking. It is but a passing dream which fades the moment you awaken to your true identity as a free independent spirit at one with the infinite All That Is, some call God.

Cherish your oneness, holding it near your heart as a mother holds her babe to her bosom. When you unite with yourself, then you will see all others through the eyes of unconditional love. It is time for an outpouring of this greater love unto humanity to awaken them from their lethargy. When enough people shine forth their radiance in the caverns of forgetfulness and ignorance, then joy will return again and hatred will be no more. The day is drawing nigh. Rejoice and know that you are one!"

I read the essay, then went to the mirror. I closed my eyes and spoke gently, "Oh, my soul, I thank you for these words of wisdom. I know I have a long way to go, but the fact that I have made contact with you gives me much hope and comfort. I do believe that I am capable of loving my self and to accept all the parts of me, both healed and unhealed and I honor the process. You remind me in this writing that 'the inner guide' is always there for us. I must turn to you when I need guidance and help. I take comfort that my rage and hatred will dissipate into the healing mist of nothingness. I pray that my heart and soul radiate fully and completely so that I can shine my light into the dark places of my own soul and into the soul of others who have forgotten. I pray to inspire them to go within and invoke their soul. To serve is my plea. As I help others, so do I heal."

I vowed that day to never deny any of my feelings and I would endeavor to learn from them each and every one, and encourage others to do the same.

Chapter Nineteen

On Creating

Over the next few days, I kept thinking about the words from *On Hatred*? that it is only when we are alienated from ourselves, that we are capable of feeling hatred for another. I realized that to know ourselves, we have to step out of denial and mental lethargy and explore our inner psyche. I was learning just how powerful the affirmation "I will to heal" is. Not only can we will to heal, but we can create any reality we wish to experience. The first step is to realize that the process of creation begins internally. A phrase popped in my head from an essay I had written years ago: "everyone's external reality is a manifestation of the inner realm of their thoughts, feelings, and desires."

I spent the rest of the day writing affirmations to help me focus on my intentions, goals, dreams and aspirations. I learned years ago that when I want something, and that "want" is backed up by strong emotions as well as action, that the desire manifests. The next morning, my divine guest added his own thoughts.

"I would like to end this little teaching seminar with the last essay you wrote shortly after leaving graduate school. It is called *On Creating*. Shall we hear it now?"

"I would be delighted, Mr. Divine."

I adjusted myself in the blue plush recliner and leaned back and closed my eyes, then began reciting.

On Creating

As you are an extension of the tao, created in Its likeness, so are you able to create. Before the creative force manifested through matter, there was the absence of the spoken word and sound. When the divine creator individualized its expression, souls were given birth and miniature gods came into being. Utilizing their inherent abilities as co-creators, cosmic energies were manipulated and material worlds formed over billions of years as measured by Earth time calculations.

Souls built material bodies to house their human ego, the mind and emotions, all of which are not original qualities of the soul. Such creation was made possible by focused, directed thought which was crystallized into concrete material form.

All creation begins in the mind where the divine ego filters its thoughts through the personality. Some of your teachers utilize the expression that "thoughts are things". This aphorism is accurate. You have but to look around to observe the worlds and individual experiences created by thought. Everyone's external reality is a manifestation of the inner realm of their thoughts, feelings, and desires. There are no exceptions. Whether one lives in material splendor and prosperity or in a condition of destitution and abject poverty depends entirely upon their mental state of mind.

All mortals possess the ability to create any material condition by simply focusing mental energy and directing thought, will, desire and most important, feeling, towards a certain end. This ability of creating is a quality of the soul; that individualized spark of divinity which is the essence of life.

Some say that only a fool would desire to live in misery. We say there are no fools. It is only foolish thinking which prevents one from creating all that would fulfill their desires. Foolish thinking is to doubt or deny the power of thought. All great inventions which have improved the living conditions of humanity would not have manifested had someone not first held the idea in mind. Today's dreamers are tomorrow's inventors!

If you wish to change your external circumstances, learn to become a dreamer; one who imagines (makes an image of) and creates in the mind. Be patient and direct mental energy to your dreams and they will begin to manifest in the outer external third dimensional world. The degree of their manifesting depends upon the amount of belief, thought and feelings given to them. Do not feel anxious or self-conscious if your friends and loved ones tease you or scoff at your dreams. Many great inventors, highly revered today, were once the object of ridicule and scoffing. Believe in the power of thought, and concentrate upon that which you desire. Imagine what it is like to touch, see, and feel the object of your desire. Give it form in your mind and spend time visualizing its essence. Be persistent and you will unleash the powers of your divine mind. Your divine mind can release invisible energy spirals capable of penetrating all vibrational frequencies and force fields of thought on very subtle levels. The divine energy is everywhere and is instantly activated by thought and will.

Focused thought and will attract this energy to you, and when there are no tinges of doubt in the mind, matter begins to coalesce, giving form to your thoughts. The creation always results from the image held in one's mind. This includes the subtle mind of the subconscious which creates dream images during sleep as well. To be an effective creator, it is important to activate and delve into the realm of the subtle mind. Creative souls such as artists, poets, and some scientists are naturally in contact with subtle mind, but all can open the door and explore the world of the subconscious and super-conscious mind.

These ideas may not be acceptable to the intellect of some people, but the intellect need not understand the subtle laws of physics which bypass even the fields of knowledge scientists have been able to penetrate. Science is slowly awakening to the realization of the reality of the sub-quantum world of subtle mind with its infinite potential for creation. There have been masters of spiritual and mystical traditions capable of performing what are called miracles. There are no miracles! To perform a miracle simply means to manipulate subtle invisible energies by the power of concentrated thought.

Believe in the unseen powers of the human mind and soul if you desire to unleash the divinity within. All are capable and destined to become co-creators with All That Is. In earlier ages, you were gods and goddesses who utilized and expressed the vast inner potential of the soul. It is unfortunate that such power finally became so abused that it destroyed human civilizations, and people were no longer able to control the divine currents. The secrets of creation must be kept from impure hearts who would manipulate divine energy for selfish purposes. The abuse of power ultimately results in destruction and death.

Purify your hearts and awaken from mortal amnesia to tap once more into the deeper layers of mind where the secrets of life and creation dwell. Become gods and goddesses once more and create peace. The days of mortal oblivion are drawing to an end. Ponder these words and remember to create only the best!"

I could not believe that I ever doubted that God and my soul were in communion with me. I would reread these essays when I was down. I vowed to make more effort to listen to my soul and follow its guidance.

Chapter Twenty

Two Soul Pleas, To Maya

It was Thursday, and the day started out rather dreary. Cold and rainy weather did nothing to diminish the "blah" feeling I woke to. Mrs. Richards had to cancel her ten a.m. appointment. Evidently, I had slept in an uncomfortable position because I had a kink in my neck. My second appointment, Jerry, was in a deep depression and we spent the hour sorting through it.

Jerry's depression seemed to linger with me after he left. Lunch was skipped as I prepared for a class – "Opening the soul's door" with a very eager group. However, a raging storm brewed just as the class began and the fierce lightning and crackling thunder seemed to have a mind of its own. When class was over, I felt as I had been the taffy in a taffy pull. A shower and a glass of wine sounded good to me.

I turned the water on as hot as I could stand. I lathered thick foamy soap over my body allowing myself to bask in the steamy warmth. The thick blue Turkish towel felt warm and comfy as I wrapped it around myself and headed towards the bedroom. I lay on my bed and the next thing I knew, I was sound asleep.

In the dream, I began creeping down the hallway. I could hear someone in my kitchen. I could see a shadow and hear glasses being taken from my cupboard. As I approached the doorway, there he was, pouring two glasses of wine at the table near the fireplace. Without looking my way, he said, "I knew you would not mind me taking the liberty of pouring the wine and joining you. I thought some wine might be nice for a change of pace or a change of drink, I should say."

I looked at Mr. Divine, so casually dressed in jeans and a Boston Red Sox sweatshirt. This was our first evening visit and I sensed that this was going to be an intense one. The entire day seemed to lead up to this. Why had I not seen the clues? I questioned myself.

We sat across from each other, rolling the wine in our glasses, the silence was never awkward, and then there it was, the beginning of the most incredible evening of my entire life. He took some sips of wine then looked into the embers of the fireplace and began.

"I apologize for the rough day that you had."

"Well, it's not your fault; it was just surprising. After all our recent talks about love and the light, I was beginning to think that my deeper wisdom would be able to help me move past the darkness. I find that my sessions with clients tend to mirror my own issues. So, when Jerry came in all despondent and in the jaws of the black beast, as he refers to his inner darkness, I sensed there was something going on with me on a deeper level. The ominous storm only mirrored that further. After he left, I think I was as depressed as he was. And the prayer we gave together, I know now, was as much for myself as for him. Sometimes I just want to give up. Sorry to sound so down, but it's how I'm feeling. It seems the more I explore my darkness, the stronger its grip becomes. Why is that?"

"Because it knows what you are up to. We have made tremendous progress in our talks. It has been very healing and insightful for you to hear those writings which have put you in touch with many inner resources of your soul. The soul is a light beacon like a lighthouse for ships. Anytime that light begins to brighten, the darkness is attracted to it and comes around. It is intensely attracted to the light because it longs to merge with it just as the light yearns to merge with the darkness. Such is natural on the worlds of duality as I have stated before.

"You have faced your darkness many times. Each experience is different just as it is for everyone. With each confrontation, your light brightens. When you name the darkness as you see it at that particular time, not as it used to be, and not what you fear it can or will become, but what IT simply IS at this time in your life, this is very empowering and angers the Darkness. One of its negative faces is that of the enraged selfish tyrant that wishes to keep you enslaved to its designs and ego hungers.

"You have stepped into the sanctuary of your soul and glimpsed the magical powers that can free you from the entanglements that further ensnare and drain your life force and gobble up your energy, joy, and your light."

My head was spinning. I felt a headache coming; fearing a migraine. I seldom got them, but when I did, they were doozies. Mr. Divine stepped closer and gently waved his hand over my face and above my head. The pain vanished. "You are getting so close to the root of your rage and then all will be seen as it is. When you totally see your darkness, it loses its power and ability to delude and manipulate you."

"I'm sorry, but this is hard to grasp. You are going way over my head. I'm not sure I can continue this conversation unless I drink an entire bottle of wine first," I said, forcing a grin.

Mr. Divine looked at me with kindness and love I had never received from anyone. He slowly lifted his half filled glass of burgundy wine. As though in a trance, totally mesmerized, I joined him in his toast: "To completely merging and submerging ourselves into the Darkness and the Light so that we can love and become them, then transcend them." We clinked glasses and took a big sip.

"I'm not sure what you mean by totally submerging and merging with the Darkness and the Light, but I fear that to do such, if it be possible, will destroy me."

"It will liberate you," he said softly.

I wanted to run out of the room and let my legs carry me as far as I could go until my body collapsed. I wanted to run so hard that my lungs would collapse. I wanted to escape. I needed to get away. This was too much to face. What did he mean by totally merging? Hadn't I done so already? What more could the darkness do to me? In how many more forms could it delude, manipulate, and attack me? I had resorted to so many devices and addictions in an effort to numb myself from its gripping painful pulls. What more could I do? I did not know, but what I did know is that I was glued to my seat and lost in Mr. Divine's compassionate loving gaze.

He looked at me as though sensing my racing thoughts. There was a long silence before he spoke again.

"Michael, listen to me carefully," he began. To fully merge with the Darkness and Light, you must step through the corridors of time and re-experience your encounters. This battle with the Darkness and the Light has been going on since the beginning of Earth time. Everyone has been involved with that battle in many lifetimes in many places and in so many roles. To be liberated, you have to call forth the 'yous' from those times and listen to their tales. See what they went through. View their struggles. Their battles. Their victories and failures. I tell you, the victory of light occurs when you come to see as I see. To see all with impartial non-judgmental eyes."

"How do I do that?

"You are already doing it to some degree. You are affected and influenced by many of those other 'yous,' both positive and negative. Your writings reveal and give glimpses of levels of awareness and enlightenment that you achieved in different lifetimes. In several, you were so close to merging totally. So close to coming fully back to the fold. So close to complete enlightenment."

"That's kind of hard to believe knowing some of the mistakes I have made in this lifetime."

"Yes, you have made mistakes as everyone else on the planet has. You take your vices and weaknesses with you in the next lifetime to correct. For example, you bring with you in this lifetime the tendency to numb your pain through alcohol, over-eating, sex, and sleep. You are even genetically predisposed to these weaknesses because members of your Earth family have some of the same weaknesses. But the good news is that just as the negative dark lives influence and affect you powerfully, (often at subconscious levels you are not aware of except when you are taken over by unexplained impulses, urges, and feelings,) so do the positive ones."

"Thank goodness for that. I just feel so lost and hopeless at times. So many times I just want to call it quits and fall into the arms of oblivion."

"Sometimes you do wish to call it quits and fall into the arms of oblivion. But not all of you does! Therein lies the key to liberation. You must remember that you are a complex person with many different sides or 'yous' as I like to call them. You must get into contact with the 'yous' that have the power and skills to help you confront, battle, and then merge with your darkness. Like a newly-wed couple, who celebrate by making love and creating new life, so can the different yous come together once more to help make you whole. The positive sub-personalities can help you with the negative ones. Human evolution is this process of merging with your own inner self, or as you put it, "Oh, my soul, at last my heart to thee do I wed!

"Most people are taught to call upon outside help when in need. There is certainly a place for this. But equally important is the need to call upon 'me,' and your 'soul' or 'true self' when in need of aid. When you feel the power of some negative sub-personality starting to take over, you have but to call upon a positive 'you' and help will be forthcoming from within. It may come from a sudden inspiration, an uplifting book or phone call out of nowhere. It can come from anywhere. The goal to experience balance and equanimity is one you have set for yourself to achieve, and you can. Almost everyone has had lifetimes where they were empowered and lived a life of balance with the darkness and the light.

"You have become weary in some lives past and given forth your various soul pleas. A strong sub-personality has had the courage to name and confront a negative one. It is time for your culture and your world to train and teach you and all Earth citizens how to meet 'the other yous or sub-personalities'."

"This sounds so far out, so crazy in a way."

"What is crazy is when you lose touch with your sub-personalities. Then they take on a life of their own and affect you subconsciously. When you experience strange moods, yearnings, anger that you cannot explain, you can be sure it originates from a sub-personality that you have lost contact with or may be denying. People can be overwhelmed by so many impulses and urges that can just appear out of nowhere with a roaring intensity, stirring up this or that hunger, longing, hurt, or fear. They can cause you to say or do things you later regret. The origins of many of these impulses come from this lifetime, but not all of them. I am telling you there is some truth to 'the multiple personality syndrome'. You all possess many personalities from many times and places, and it is the lack of integration of these personalities that contributes to insanity, craziness, and mental illness. Such troubled people are often drugged to numb them so they do not have to deal with their sub-personalities."

"My friend and therapist, Elizabeth used to say, 'If you don't deal with the inner pain, then you have to numb it.'"

"Unfortunately, that is the road so easily taken by your psychiatrists and doctors. The repression and numbing of the sub-personalities is what creates neurosis or even psychosis. Obsessive compulsive behaviors, addictions, depression and a load of other maladies could all be cured if you got in touch with your sub-personalities more. They are your inner self/selves, or aspects of your soul self which make up your complete inner family. There are many ways to contact them. It occurs in dreams. It can be done through hypnotherapy, talking to yourself, through meditation, journaling, active imagination exercises, divination, music, or through art.

"One means you utilize is 'writing'. You think you are making something up, or channeling spirits when often you are simply contacting another 'you'. For example, when you decided to leave your doctoral program in French, your soul was so delighted that you were not going to sell out on your writing dream, that another 'you' stepped forth and showed you yet another fascinating aspect of yourself. You wrote a whole new series of 'writings' rich in insight.

"Now, let us meet that 'you,' in two of your writings: *Two Soul Pleas* and *To Maya*. You wrote, or better put, another 'you' or sub-personality wrote those two beautiful pieces shortly after you agreed to leave graduate school. Let's hear them now."

"Yes," I said softly. "I recall how peaceful I felt while writing them. I did not care if the world fell apart or the sky fell on us. I am filled with serenity and joy when I write such things.

Nothing can disturb my equilibrium then."

Mr. Divine took another sip of wine then smiled and asked me if I'd like another glass of wine. It was tempting, but I said no. "Well, if you do not mind, I think I will," he said, with a mischievous glow in his eyes. After he sat back down and took his first sip, I began speaking.

Two Soul Pleas

Caught up in the whirlwind of Maya's perpetual motion, I spin and spin. From one cycle to the next, I taste the fruit of action and reaction, sometimes bitter, sometimes sweet, but never does it satisfy. Oh, my soul, deliver me from Illusion's spin!

Tight is Maya's grip upon me. Oh, my soul, help me extricate myself from her suffocating grasp. Her devouring form weighs heavily upon me. I pray thee, oh, my soul, grant me release. Maya is like a wild beast clawing away at my heart. Only you can save me from her savage attacks. Without your divine shelter, she will catch me then rip away life, tearing me into bits and pieces.

You are immune to Maya's poisonous darts. Oh, my soul, may I take shelter in your arms and rest at your breast? I beg thee, hear my cry and extend your loving mercy!

To Maya

As I look around me, what do I see? Restless, hungry souls trapped inside bodies which continuously torture them with transient pleasures which do not console the heart or soul. Ephemeral mundane satiations temporarily fill the deep inner void, while deceiving me once more to believe I can truly enjoy the passionate dance with the flesh.

The nocturnal pleasures fade with the breath of each new dawn and once more the soul is filled with an even deeper emptiness. The sensitive spirit gazes into the eyes of those about and sees what they cannot see themselves. He hears the cry of their hearts begging to be released from Illusion's dark lonely pit.

Maya, oh vile mistress of deception! Your seductive
embrace lures us to your lusty chambers. Your poisonous sweet
lips suck away our life force. Your tantalizing whispers enchant
us, and we walk into your trap with eyes closed, unable to view
the warning sign, "Step not into the chamber of grief and woe!"
How many times have I been your victim, relinquishing my free
will yet once more for another night with you?

Maya, goddess of misfortune, you offer joy and pleasure, but
at the price of constant ravaging and gnawing at my soul. With
each indulgence, I become weaker and you become stronger. The
times I avoid you, other victims satisfy your insatiable hunger for
immortality, granting you another day of life. Immortality you
will attain, you say, but a soft voice tells me, "Not so! Maya lives
only as long as we allow. Her days are numbered. Withdraw
from her embrace and her power is diminished."

Wretched, Maya, release me from your clutches. Sink back
to your abyss of death and deception. My soul is weary, but not
extinguished.   My spirit has succumbed to your subtle
temptations, but the faint whispers of my soul awaken and stir
memories I have never been able to completely forget – memories
of the part of me you cannot penetrate nor seduce; the part of me
who is indifferent to your soft caresses; the part of me that can
destroy you.

Maya, you are but a dream! A mirage that will disappear the
moment I refuse to behold your fleeting form. Phantom of the
dark, flee! I have seen the night. The moment is nigh. It is time
to approach the light!

"It is time to approach the light," I whispered. I closed my
eyes and lost myself into the memory and power of this writing.
A half hour must have passed before Mr. Divine tapped me gently
on the knee and spoke.

"Welcome back, gentle monk," he said softly. "Some of
your most peaceful lifetimes have been spent as a monk."

I was speechless and nearly breathless as well. It was one
thing to have some psychic tell you that you have been a monk in
another lifetime, but quite another to have my divine guest

confirm it. My mind went back to childhood before we left for foster homes. My spirituality has always been very important to me even at a young age. I could accept the notion that I had been a monk in some past lives. Several psychics had told me that in readings. My thoughts continued to wander a few moments more then Mr. Divine brought me back to the moment.

"Your words come straight from the heart and soul," Mr. Divine said, pointing to my heart. "You have been monks in both the East and West so naturally, your writing reflects both styles. Maya, as you know, is the goddess of Illusion in the eastern teachings. Your writings also have the flavor of some of the psalms of David."

"David," I exclaimed. "I have always been drawn to him and my favorite biblical passage is The 23rd Psalm. I memorized it many years ago and recite it often."

"It is a beautiful Psalm that appeals to me enormously. I recommend that you call upon this monk sub-personality when you are feeling despair and wanting to give up as you said earlier. He is as much a part of your 'total self' as the despairing ones. You challenge Maya and Her illusions in the writing. You admit to having succumbed to her temptations, but also acknowledge the part of yourself that is indifferent to her and that can destroy her. Well, you can never really destroy her, but you can diminish or nullify her hold onto you. You can transcend Maya to the degree that you wish and your monk sub-personalities are very qualified to help you accomplish this goal. I say to the degree that you wish because if you totally renounced mortal illusion, you could not exist or function on the planes of duality at all.

"Enlightenment need not be hurried. Take your time. You must be ready to relinquish your attachments before such can transpire. Does this make sense?"

"Somewhat. I know the monk part of me. I knew about him many years ago without really knowing I knew. I will never forget that time when I was studying in France. Aside from the fact that I had deja-vu often in France, one experience has never left me. We were visiting the Roman ruins in the southern part of France. I wandered off and discovered this old French monastery. When the monks welcomed me, I was filled with a sense of calm and peace. I wanted to stay in that place and never leave. My mind kept telling me I was being totally irrational because at that time, I was going through my agnostic stage. Yet my heart felt such a connection to those monks. In some way, it felt like coming home."

"And you did come back home; to a home and place that another sub-personality from another time cherished long ago. Such powerful emotional reactions that defy rhyme and reason are often a good indicator that some circumstance has called up another sub-personality. It would be easy for you to become that monk again and renounce the pleasures of the flesh and the world."

"When I moved in with the monks in the Hare Krishna temple in 1991 for six months, I seriously considered becoming a monk. We chanted, studied and lived the simple life; I was never happier. It was even a delight to scrub the pots and pans and serve the people who came for the free Sunday night feast. I have been told that I have been a monk in India twice, once in Tibet, twice in Italy and a friar in France twice."

"That is accurate and the regressions and past life readings you had are accurate as well."

"I find it fascinating that psychics who never met me could tell me about monk lives in France and Italy. Those were my two favorite countries when I studied and traveled in Europe. French was so easy for me to learn and I even taught myself Italian. I memorized the *St. Francis Prayer for Peace* years ago and say it all the time."

"You are invoking another sub-personality, a past life monk, when you do this. One day, everyone will be able to invoke their positive sub-personalities to come to their rescue when facing hardships. Who do you think helped you detach yourself from your material life before you moved in the temple for six months back in 1990? Once you made the decision to leave your Ph.D. program, within a week you moved from your apartment, got rid of all your French books, filed for bankruptcy, and started over."

"Do you have to bring the bankruptcy up? I'm still

embarrassed about that."

"You have moved on, Michael. You started over then and the bankruptcy was all part of the clearing out. You can call it a period of major 'house cleaning' if that makes you feel better. You have since completely rebuilt your credit, paid off your student loan and credit cards, and even have some money put away. If you learn from your mistakes in life, you are not bound to repeat them. The monk sub-personality gave you the strength and courage to start over. You lived very simply for several years. You had been strongly immersed into the drama of the material world; it was simply time to withdraw, reflect, and start a new course and direction in life. Your monk sub-personality led you many steps of the way as he is doing now. You do not have a regular job with a normal salary, benefits, insurance and such. You look in your calendar and sometimes you have nothing booked for an entire month. But you always have what you need when you need it. You live by faith and surrender to your spiritual mission which is to help others. Your calendar always has a way of getting booked, does it not?"

"Yes, but sometimes I get a little nervous."

"That keeps you humble. You truly are doing what you love and the money is always there. You know this. The monk part of you knows this just as he knew it when you were a Franciscan monk back in France."

"It has been a few years ago since I decided to do the spiritual counseling full time. I recall spending my last few dollars on some ads which didn't bring me a single client. I even had to borrow rent money that month. I guess I was being tested?"

"Yes, in a sense, and you did not sell out and go back to teaching. You kept plugging away, never giving up on your dream and desire to serve through your counseling, spiritual work and your writing."

"I sure have felt like giving up so many times. More than once I considered going back to teaching or re-opening my tutoring and singing telegram business. Money was so tight then."

"Almost everyone has felt like giving up at some time or another. That is no reason for guilt or shame. What is important is that in spite of your trials, tests, and tribulations, you hang in there. And that is what you have done. This makes you a fine example and a qualified mentor to others. You hung in there and stayed true to your dream. The monk part of you fed your soul with faith and inspiration and helped you to stick it out. Little by little, doors began to open, and now you are faring much better, are you not?"

"Yes. It was very tough giving up a teaching career to be a psychic/spiritual counselor pursuing a writing dream on the side; I must admit that it was sheer hell at times. The uncertainty, the bills piling up, the phone not ringing, and the fear of starving which I have been told stems from a couple lifetimes where that actually did happen."

"And you got through it all."

"I got through it all and still am. After I realized I did not want to become a full time monk, I told a friend I needed a new place to live. She just happened to have a friend who enjoyed being around writers and artists. She had a spare third floor apartment in her enormous house and let them live there in exchange for some help around the house. My good fortune was that her present occupant just happened to be moving within the week. Elizabeth took me to meet the couple and a week later, I was moved in. So I do know what you are talking about."

"You know there is really no such thing as good fortune. Call it your good karma, if you will, that sent that opportunity your way. You had been working hard at your writing dream and it was your destiny to be rewarded with that temporary live-in situation with that couple."

"I was very grateful for that. That was a very healing time of growing for me. I lived in a mansion with a rich couple. I remember glowing like a light bulb that day I found a dime on my car seat floor mat."

"That was true renunciation, Michael."

"I was like a kid in a candy store wanting to know what all I could buy with my dime. Then, six months later, their condo was finished and it was time to move on again. Can you believe that I actually packed my books a month in advance and started affirming that an agreeable place to live would turn up?"

"Yes, you believed and knew beforehand just like Jesus gave thanks for the fish and bread knowing that it was already done. This is a quality that you have internalized from your monk lives."

"Well, part of me was scared I'd wind up on the street, in a shelter or YMCA, or heaven knows where. I had a hunch a few days later to visit a friend who was running two businesses. Her room-mate had moved out a few weeks before and she was agreeable to having me move into the spare room if I'd run errands and help her around the house. That was a close one. I had even put some ads in the paper advertising house cleaning or yard and outside work offered in exchange for room and board. Nothing turned up although I did get a few calls."

"You were willing to do whatever it took to keep body and soul together as long as you had time for writing. This is a struggle you are very familiar with and you knew on a soul level that you had to move past your fears and push forward. You gave up in your last life, and one of your challenges for this one has been not to give up, no matter what."

"I guess better later than never, as the saying goes. At least I finally got my first book published two years ago."

"Each accomplishment paves the way for additional ones. You worked very hard on *Halfway to Heaven* and you deserve the recognition you got, but that is but the mere beginning."

"I guess as my friend Elizabeth always said, 'More to come.'"

"More to come is right. The 'yous' of yesterdays and yester lives and future lives are not grave bound by any means. They are alive and well in your soul and psyche. You have far more contact with them than you can imagine, though much of it is unconscious. You all affect and influence each other in ways you can hardly imagine or even fathom. Your soul knows more of your greater being and picture. It knows of the 'yous' that have already lived on the Earth, currently live on the Earth, and who will live on the Earth. It knows of the yous that have lived on other planets, and the 'yous' that have inhabited many forms not human, but of finer, ethereal essence, and of your experiences as pure free spirit."

"Mr. Divine, please pardon me, but some people would consider such talk just drug induced hallucinations or something similar."

"Let them think as they will. It takes nothing away from the truth. Yes, it is true that some people do take drugs to tap into the sea of their greater being. However, it is not a path that I recommend for the most part. The direction I am heading in may sound far out or even imaginative, but I assure you, Michael that you can relate far more to what I am saying. You have had many experiences that I refer to as 'transcendental' and you even wrote a very nice little piece many years ago called *Transcendence*.

"I vaguely recall that one."

"It is lovely I might add and I'd like to suggest that you dig it out and reread it. We can talk about it in our next visit. Now it is time for me to take my leave."

"Good bye, Mr. Divine."

"Until next time," he said, then vanished.

Chapter Twenty-One

Transcendence

I thought about Mr. Divine saying I had had many experiences that he referred to as "transcendental." I found my little book and turned to *Transcendence*.

Transcendence

I can no longer define the world according to the limited mortal vision that has blinded me from reality far too long. It is time to open the windows of the soul and look within so the external realm can be seen and understood more clearly.

The blinding mist of ignorance must now dissipate. It is time to perceive those absolute realities which do not change; time to look deeper within until I behold the divine spark which animates life; time to taste the immortal ambrosia from the divine banquet; time to partake of its sumptuous delights so my spirit will know satisfaction and peace. I must know the secrets which lie beyond mortal comprehension.

There is a center within my being which carries the seed of transcendental knowledge, and the essence of all life. This center animates my every yearning and hunger to experience the divine within the heart. These invisible minute spirals of energy permeate every atom and cell of my being. Moving in circular motion, they will activate the divine consciousness that the immortal spirit spark planted deep within my soul by All That Is the great creator of us all.

Spirit and Matter will unite when we choose to remember who we truly are. It is time for sleepy mortals to awaken from their material dreams and renounce the delusions which entangle them in the web of forgetfulness. We must shake ourselves out of this drunken stupor and claim our identity as sons and daughters of the infinite All That Is.

This lowly abode of mortal illusion is not the natural dwelling of the soul. I have been living a nightmare on Terra, chasing phantoms and ghouls who only exist in my imagination because I have forgotten what is real.

No more slumbering in this mortal chamber where the black mist of oblivion shrouds my spirit. No more closing my eyes to the vast realms of infinite bliss. I am a part of All That Is, and All That Is is a part of me.

It is time for the secrets of the soul to be revealed. I listen for your voice!

I thought about that writing the rest of the day. It was still on my mind that night when I went to bed. I was bedazzled how such words just popped out of nowhere. I fell asleep wondering if I would ever see them in print.

Mr. Divine showed up before dawn the next morning. We had a wonderful steaming cup of coffee, then he spoke to me.

"Did you enjoy rereading *Transcendence?*"

"Yes, I guess I can get pretty deep at times."

"You sure can."

"It sounds like being human was not easy on that particular day."

"Being human is not easy as long as you are estranged and alienated from your soul. Divinity and mortality are destined to dance together, not be alienated from each other. Your soul was literally jumping out at you through those words, hoping you could sense its presence. Your soul was inviting you to bond and reunite with it, or to put more poetically, it was inviting you to dance."

"I seem to keep saying the same things over and over in different writings. The readers are going to get bored."

"Repetition is necessary. It is not easy conveying such ideas, so you say them in different ways in different writings. In spite of the sad fact that most people are vaguely, if at all, aware of their soul on a conscious level, unconsciously everyone is aligned. Writers, poets, artists, philosophers, musicians, you name it, are all speaking the wisdom of the soul, whether portraying it via sound, words, colors, or what have you. No other words are sweeter and your soul is working very hard at taking you to deeper and more profound understandings. There is purpose and meaning in your human experience, but it is your soul who can teach you that and guide you through your human journey. These beautiful 'writings' that you have been sharing, come from deep within and are meant to remind you and others of 'your greater being' and 'your greater picture'."

"Sometimes, I think delving into my greater being is going to drive me over the edge and land me in a nuthouse."

"Yes, this can be overwhelming to the ego at times. There is a need to assimilate, integrate and synthesize. You do need to slow down, take breaks, and do things to keep grounded. We don't want you blowing any neural circuitry here."

"Yesterday, it got real intense, so by 4 p.m., I just stopped writing for the day and went to my sister's to enjoy their farm. That was hard though because a million thoughts were rushing through my mind. Nature always has a way of calming me down. I'm glad I went. Now, here we are at it again."

"Yes, we are at it again. I'm having a lovely time sipping coffee, enjoying the crackling fireplace, gazing into the embers and being reminded that the pure fire in your soul is helping you to burn away the impurities of your limited human thinking and perceptions that keep you enslaved to your passions. People love the fire because it reflects the pristine light of their own soul. The soul's essence is that of pure light and to behold its glowing, scintillating radiance is a wonder that never ceases to warm the heart and enchant the mind and emotions."

"I've always had this thing for candles, fireplaces, campfires and such. In a meditation years ago, a goddess with coal black hair and emerald glowing eyes came to me. She said her name was Dresda. Although my eyes were closed, I could see her as clearly as I see you here now. Her words to me were:

"I am flame. I am fire.
I set in motion the heart's desire."

"What beautiful words. Dresda is a muse and a goddess who dwells on a higher plane. You are wise to invoke her when you need guidance, and support. You have had lives with her in other times and in spirit lands that make this human experience look like kid stuff as the saying goes."

"I did feel an instant connection and deep love for her. I even wrote a story about Dresda. It's in some pile gathering dust."

"She will forgive you."

"I think it was Dresda who used to whisper to me that I had to hang in there when I wanted to give up. I used to want to exit this body, but now I know I have more to accomplish."

"Yes there is yet much for you to accomplish on the Earth."

"I am reminded of that old song from the seventies, 'O Happy Day!' What a Happy Day that will truly be when I am done here."

"It will be a happy day for you and then you can march to the cadence of life's dance as you wish."

"That sounds familiar. Didn't I write something about that just recently?"

"Maybe," Mr. Divine said, pointing and waving a finger to me in jest.

"Yes, it was in Florida. I remember now. I was walking around a resort and got lost in the beauty of the ferns, flowers, bushes and trees. It looked like a veritable Eden. I even said I'd like to move to Florida. My actual words were, 'I'd even sweep sidewalks at Disney world, if I could come home at night to such beauty.' When I saw the fireworks, I simply wanted to fly away. At three a.m. when my friends were fast asleep soaring in their own dreams I wrote *Spirit March*. It is still in my notebook and I have not looked at it since. My out of sight, out of mind thing can make me look like a total amnesiac."

"I would love to hear it."

"Me too. I have it memorized as it's only two paragraphs long," I said and then began softly reciting.

Spirit March

There was a time not so very long ago when our vibrant spirits danced and soared on the tails of galaxies. Our wings carried us to unimaginable flights of destiny. With each golden magical moment our dreams and hopes soared beyond mortal illusions, and we glimpsed something so entrancing, so enchanting that we sighed in awe and wonder as our souls soared higher and higher. Then we beheld a tiny sparkling star.

Its scintillating golden radiance filled us with delight and we were lost in total childlike wonder. We lifted our arms, wings gliding higher and higher until we stepped beyond this world and entered other domains. Spirits flew and came to greet us. Hand in hand, wings in full iridescent extension, we soared and we flew. Time smiled lovingly upon us. We slowly descended. Our feet made their way to the ground. Our eyes twinkled as our hearts beat softly to the music of the spheres. A perfect cadence. One rhythm. We glided effortlessly singing and dancing to the spirit march!

"Nice."

"I had all but forgotten I wrote it and that was not even two months ago."

"Now perhaps you realize why you often have flying dreams."

"They seem so real; I've had them all of my life. Even when I ran so much in college, I'd get lost. Sometimes I'd look up at the sky and it truly felt like I could soar. I guess dance and movement are the body's means of attempting to fly to meet the soul."

"Something like that. It is certainly not meant for the body to be sedentary. Everyone needs daily exercise."

"So tell me, are the raging fires in my soul a good or bad thing?"

"Neither, in and of themselves. They are pure energy and energy moves in either positive or negative directions, sometimes both. Your anger is not a bad thing. We will get into that tomorrow. For now, I want you to bask in that wonderful energy you felt when you wrote *Spirit March,* so I will take my leave."

"Maybe I'll have flying dreams tonight."

"You never know."

Chapter Twenty-Two

The Healing Power of Anger

I did have flying dreams; it seemed they lasted all night, but they could not have because I was greeted early the next morning by my divine guest with a mug of steaming French Vanilla coffee. We engaged in small talk a few minutes, then he picked up where he left off in our conversation yesterday.

"Like I said yesterday, anger is not a bad thing. It can propel you to greater knowing and awareness and action. It is an aspect of the darkness that can serve you. Acknowledging it dissipates much of its negative destructive energy. If you recall, you were speaking about your anger just a couple of weeks ago with your friend Karen. You told her you were not sure what was at the bottom of it, and you said something else more important. You said that you wanted to understand and get to its origins. Much like your 'pomp' peace of mind plea, you prayed your 'anger origins prayer'. Why don't you tell me what happened?"

"I got some insight, didn't I?"

"Yes because to ask is to receive. You have struggled with your anger and rage for so long; sadly it never occurred to you to go to your greatest teacher, your soul, to whom you have prayed so often before the phrase, "Oh, my soul! Show me the way!" The origins of your anger stem from more than one source and definitely from more than one lifetime. There is a definite theme that has prevailed in many of them: the feeling of being trapped in a physical body, for in your heart of hearts, you know that you are star borne."

I shivered. "You give me cold chills when you say that. I can recall having this feeling as a child like a cat chasing its tail. Sometimes, I'd spin around and around in circles trying to catch my self. I felt that part of me was missing, and just like a cat or dog will keep running around trying to catch its tail, I felt that if

I ran long and fast enough I could catch the rest of me. I know this sounds silly, but I had that little fantasy for years; except it was more than that. I'd actually stand up tall, try to put my feet in firm steady stance, and then I'd start spinning around. Faster I'd go until, like the song *Ring around the Rosie*, I'd fall down. But I always got back up and my eyes always found their way to the stars, and I longed to be up there."

"Even as a child you wanted to escape your physical limitations. Why do you think children love airplane games? Your nieces used to beg you to play with them. 'Lift me up,' they would say, their little arms flinging in the air, pretending to be airplanes. Why do you think the airplane was invented in the first place? Mankind knew in his soul that he was destined to fly. Since he could not endow himself with physical wings he did the next best thing and created a big giant bird machine that enabled him to soar."

"That makes sense. Can you tell more about the insight I got when I invoked my 'anger origins prayer.'"

"I can, but I invite you to speak first. After you and your friend were talking about your inexplicable anger, she went out with a friend. Alone in your hotel room, you thought about your anger. How it has gotten you into trouble, but never into deep trouble because you have always been in touch with it, and did your utmost to keep tabs on it and to control it."

"I haven't always done the best job at controlling my temper and my anger."

"Well, let's just say you could have done much worse. You have at least been able to dissipate some of your rage's destructive energy by admitting and naming it and doing your best to find some suitable healthy outlets for it such as jogging, writing, and singing."

"Yeah, my poor mother kept her rage inside for years until it finally exploded, resulting in a stroke; my father had a heart attack. My oldest brother died of a massive heart attack at age 49 from so much hurt of the heart and repressed pain and anger. His heart was broken. At least I did not become a stark raving maniac and kill someone such as we are seeing more and more with the killing rampages that are taking place all over the world. But I confess, there were times I feared I might. I sure had some pretty weird and scary fantasies sometimes."

"Yes, but fantasies are not the same thing as physical actions. Actually, an active fantasy life is what has kept you from going over the edge. Psychologists have much to learn about the healing that active fantasies have to offer. Most people freak out when they have morbid cruel fantasies and do everything to repress them. This only feeds and fuels their rage more. Continued repression can turn the person into a monster who at some point, does act out their fantasies. You have been fortunate enough to have some extraordinary therapists and counselors who encouraged you to explore your fantasies.

"By openly acknowledging them, you were in a position to learn why they were there and what they were about. There is much more symbolic essence and meaning to fantasy than most people realize. You have had much help in this regard and fortunately, you have not gone over the edge. You never will as long as you don't deny and repress your anger, rage and you continually find creative outlets for those powerful energies."

"You sound like a shrink."

"I don't mind being a shrink from time to time."

"This is rather fascinating and I hope to explore this topic further at a future talk, but let's get back to that insight I got."

"After Karen left, you thought about your anger, and then you had a spontaneous urge to take out your notebook and write. You called your little writing *Anger*. Shall we hear that now?"

"Sure."

Anger

You ask me why I am angry. I will tell you. Anger is the only passionate emotion that can shake me temporarily from my state of detachment that makes my hold on this mortal life so tenuous, so fragile. Anger makes me forget for awhile what I know in the innermost reaches and depths of my soul and heart – that nothing – no thing is truly real or has any significance or meaning other than what I assign to it in the grander scheme of my total being.

I taste, smell, see, hear and feel with my five physical senses, groping for a tighter grip, a firmer grasp on what reality truly is, and I know that it is all ephemeral, temporary, fading and misty much like the evanescent floating images that appear to me in night slumber. And yet I pretend it is real. I must if I am to continue to exist on this plane, and all it requires is that one small part of my soul convinces itself that the human design is worthwhile and meaningful.

Words of a madman? Perhaps, but perhaps words of a weary traveler who knows the Earth is not his place of origin that he can truly call home. Without this realization, he cannot even take in the breath of life that pours into him so hungrily, so demanding that he fill his corporeal essence with this life force and take his place in the world.

Why does he dance alone in the darkness? Let his limbs move with listless robotic monotony? Because he knows there is no true or permanent order or harmony in this small world of relativity, and he is not sure that permanence exists either. He can only perceive that there is something true and ever lasting outside his limited field of vision. With determination and willful persistence, he yearns and hopes to tap into realities beyond his comprehension and this realm.

He can only hope there is meaning he can glimpse and perhaps even grasp that stems from deeper levels of awareness. These eyes of mine are but a meager tool allowing me to truly see and know that which I see. Their purpose is to help me define and name images which my retina reveal as true of form, whose essence is worth examining.

Words of a babbling fool? You may think so, but I am not so sure. Before you dismiss me as a madman, I invite you to ponder and examine these words and ideas thoroughly. That is all I ask of you as that is all that I ask of myself!

We were quiet a few moments. Mr. Divine played with his pony tail for a minute, then took a big swig of water from the glass he had poured earlier. I did the same, then spoke. "It seems I'm pretty pissed off at being here on the Earth. Is that the origin of my anger?"

"It is the origin of some of your anger. In this writing, you are back to fighting Maya, that Goddess of Illusion. Let me tell you a secret. Maya dwells inside of you as well as outside of you. She is both real and not real as is everything on the planes of duality such as we have discussed before. Maya does dwell in the center of your being, but she is not the center of your being."

"That is very interesting. My friend emailed me this morning and offered a little prayer for me: 'Maya, find your center. Dwell within it and become brave.' This is like telling the wave to bask in the ripples that toss and send it back to the ocean. How can it be sent to something outside itself since the wave is not the ocean?"

"It is the ocean if you view it from the absolute realm. You say that anger makes you forget that nothing is real. How profound, yet more profound is the fact that your anger is not real either. It, like everything else in your world, can only have the meanings you assign to it. You have chosen to become involved with the many people and have created or shall I say co-created each and every experience with all of them. You have gotten lost in the various mazes and labyrinths and you have chosen to do that so you could experience confusion and the anger that results from not having your desires fulfilled. Of course you, like everyone, have created each of your attachments and the desires behind them. A master lives in a state of involved detachment. Having no attachment to outcomes, nothing can upset a master's equilibrium. To reach that state is to attain equanimity and bliss."

"Whew, this is some heavy stuff here. I think I'm getting lost."

"You can only escape the labyrinth when you realize you are lost in it. Otherwise said, you escape the need for escape and being lost when you realize you were never lost to begin with, but you only thought you were."

"Oh no, are we going on another wild goose chase?"

"Let me try to simplify. Bear with me because words are in and of themselves very poor tools to convey such concepts. On the most absolute realm, there is no duality, so the human experience can make no sense since to be human is to be dualistic on a 'relative' world. As divinity and spirit coalesce with matter, then the light of the absolute begins to dim and the soul begins to glimpse and perceive other lights and other energies and vibrations. As the brilliance of the soul light dims, its vibratory rate decelerates more and more until it is able to align itself with the level of vibratory energy that you call third dimensional density or matter.

"At this point, divinity has now divided itself into countless sparks and soul lights much like the stars that grace your night skies. The soul light shines, but the amount of density it aligns itself with determines the radiance of its glow and what kind of experiences it will attract. Part of partaking of density and the third dimension is to step into the realm of the relative where time and space exist on a probable level. The soul never truly accepts or believes this, but it humors the ego all the while knowing that its involvement with the ego expands the soul's understanding and learning. In this regard, the human experience does have meaning.

"Part of your anger is because of the division created within your soul's own sphere; meaning that to participate in the human experiment it had to dim its light enough to entrap a part of itself in human density. The soul knows it can never be separate from All That Is, but the ego thinks that it can. Healing this rift is what evolution is about. Through its willingness to interact with the ego, it finds itself in all kinds of strange settings, bodies, and circumstances on all types of worlds, planets, and other galaxies and universes.

"The soul has gone along with the ego for its many and diverse rides across the cosmos over the centuries. But like the prodigal son who never forgets his connection to his father, after so long, it becomes bored and restless. It can never be completely devoid of soul light no matter how heavily involved it becomes in mortality and being human. Some believe the soul light can be extinguished, but I say that is a fallacy. It can transmute into other types of energy and light, and experience a more ethereal or spiritual version of itself. But destroyed, never. Energy is never created or destroyed as your physicists say, it is merely transformed.

"One of the things your anger and pain can do is to shove open the door to your soul whose light of understanding and truth can permeate it. This is why some of your mystics and more creative souls speak of having some of their most potent breakthroughs into deeper understanding and truth after agonizing dark nights of the soul. When the darkness becomes so dense and heavy that you fear extinction, if there is a sincere plea and prayer to God, the higher self, the soul, whatever words you choose, then the light of the soul actually extends itself outward into the subtle spheres of your being and draws the darkness towards it to merge with it. The result is what some call the feeling of being immersed into 'the great white light'. This outpouring of light, which is accompanied by ineffable joy or bliss, is also referred to as being filled with the 'holy ghost.' Some refer to the experience as the opening of 'the crown chakra' into super-consciousness or complete God or soul awareness. As you know, words are poor tools to express such concepts, but until humanity evolves further, words are what we have to work with at this time."

"I understand. No wonder the eastern symbol of the yin and yang of the light and dark is so special to me. The light and darkness do merge."

"If this merging did not occur, the glow of your soul would be so bright that it would be totally beyond your grasp or perceptions. It must intertwine with your darkness before its divine light can penetrate your being and awaken or 'enlighten' your higher self who is the intermediary between ego and soul or pure 'spirit'. There must be the merging with the darkness before you can be immersed in 'the great white light' or be filled with 'the holy ghost'. There must be a balance between your light and your darkness.

"Your higher, greater self or soul knows that your anger is part of your darkness. It is one of your great teachers, and along with despair, and depression, it is a very demanding and difficult teacher. It will only move to the light if you surrender your hold to your ego and take the journey into your own personal abyss. Unlike what most people think, the way to the light is to move through the darkness. You must face your inner darkness before you can heal and become enlightened."

"As a matter of fact, I have recently been re-reading a book, *Meeting the Shadow,* that deals with this very topic. The quote on the back cover by Carl G. Jung says it perfectly. "One does not become enlightened by imagining figures of light, but by making the darkness conscious.""

"Carl Jung was a wise man. Most people are unhappy because they either do not believe or understand this concept. Nor have they made their darkness conscious. Most try to do the very opposite and they fear the dark domain of their unconscious mind. Some even deny that they have an unconscious mind, although dreams ought to prove the contrary.

"As you meet and face your darkness via 'the dark nights of the soul' as this journey has been referred to by mystics, then your crown chakra, or the higher mind, is filled with divine luminescence. At the highest achievement of this level of spiritual alchemy, you become what is called an avatar, God-incarnate, or a Buddah. At this level, one has complete mastery over self/selves and can perform what are commonly referred to as miraculous acts. The darkness and the light have totally merged.

"To know how much divine light is lacking, or to what degree the soul is dancing with density, to use a poetic expression, in these variable 'yous' it is important to learn more about these 'yous'. As I said earlier, there are many 'yous' alive and well, living in what you call the past, and the future. On a higher level, the present is the one place and moment where they join hands and celebrate their oneness and total unity. They also contain their own 'darkness' and past life regressions and hypnosis can be helpful tools to connect with them.

"Part of your deep seated anger is due to old hurts and unresolved conflicts from some of those lifetimes, and although you may be unconscious of them, they still affect you and contribute to the causes and creations of your deepest impulses, fears, phobias, talents, abilities, and other human characteristics. Actually, it is the unresolved conflicts and struggles (karma as many refer to it) that you take to the grave after the termination of each physical incarnation that determines the place and circumstances of your future incarnations.

"The truth is that 'self' can never hide from 'self'. The ego can pretend or ignore its pains and hurts and the hurts and pain it has inflicted upon others, but the soul has access to all its lives. It knows that the amount of light it can dispense to lead the ego out of the darkness depends upon how well the ego learns from and corrects the mistakes made in the many lives it has lived. The work must be done or as some say the piper must be paid. No cheating is allowed. It is such self delusion and cheating that accounts for so much human misery.

"Lessons avoided become more difficult in each additional lifetime. Anger shoved down and repressed only magnifies and intensifies until it can explode into booming rage which can become as a volcano consuming and destroying anyone and anything in its path. I might add that not all of your anger or love originates from your Earth lives. One cannot know great rage, pain or hurt if they have not equally known, experienced and expressed great love. I have said enough for now. I want you to ponder these thoughts until we next meet."

"Thank you. You have given me much to ponder."

"The pleasure is always mine."

Chapter Twenty-Three

Fantasy Possesses Elements of Truth

I did not hear from Mr. Divine for the next few days. I sensed that our visits were coming to an end, but I dared not mention this as I hoped that my intuition was wrong. I tried to think of what topics I'd like for him yet to cover; nothing came to mind.

To divert myself, I dug out my old copy of the Stephen King Dark Tower IV novel, *Wizard and Glass*, and tried to lose myself in his main character, the Gunslinger's world. Although I enjoyed the story, I still found myself nervous and edgy. Reading fantasy novels was now stirring up something deep inside that I could not quite understand. I would ask Mr. Divine about it.

The next day he showed up dressed in a baseball outfit, complete with "Boston Red Socks" hat and a pair of red-spiked shoes. It took all my attention to keep from bursting out laughing. With his hair tucked under his hat, I had to admit that he looked real cute – well, cute is the only word I could think of to describe him. I tried to imagine him on the field playing ball and I could just hear all the girls cheering him on – and the guys as well.

I could not resist asking why he wore a baseball outfit.

"On the one hand, life itself is one big game. I thought I would dress the part for one of your more popular ones."

"Oh, I see."

"I chose the look of 'The Boston Red socks' for my team because you have some special memories of Boston. Don't you think I look cool?"

"You look super-cool, Mr. Divine, even if this is only a dream."

"Only a dream," he repeated then winked at me. "And what dreams may come." He smiled, then became quiet. I prepared our morning coffee and we enjoyed it in the silence. After I poured our second cup, he gave me a serious look. I could feel my heart beginning to race. Was he going to blast my grip on reality today? A thin smile came across his face and then he began.

"Michael, I am aware of your restlessness. Let me say that your higher mind is more active than normal as of late; it is endeavoring to teach you some things which might be difficult for you to assimilate or even believe. Do you know why it takes you so long to write your fantasy novels? Do you know why it took five years to finish your first one? Do you know why you have ideas for dozens of fantasy and science-fiction short stories which you have never written, and many others that you started but never completed? Do you know why you have not finished your book, *The Wonderful World of What Ifs?* It is because its basic premise unsettled you. You felt your grip and grasp on reality might collapse should you dive wholeheartedly into such an endeavor. You have a difficult time being a fantasy writer because of a discrepancy of what your soul knows to be true and what your mind has been told about fantasy. Michael, now it is time that we talked more in depth about truth and fantasy. Do you want to hear something mind-blowing?"

"Sure, why not," I replied, "as you could probably tell by the look on my face, I have been bitten by the apathy bug as of late. Go, ahead, rock my world again."

"Before I do that, let's talk about your interest in fantasy stories. Would you care to begin?"

"Well, let's see. I've had an interest in fantasy stories ever since I can remember. I was so hooked on C.S. Lewis' *Chronicles of Narnia* my freshman year of college that I hid in the basement bathroom lobby so I could read, undisturbed. Time simply stops and I get lost in those other worlds that seem so real. I experienced similar feelings when I wrote my own fantasy stories, and my one and only fantasy novel – so far – *Rolana's Awakening"*

"What else did you observe as you read and lost yourself in those other worlds?"

"That I was never depressed. Maybe that's why people call

soap operas and novels a means to escape everyday life."

"I am here to tell you, Michael, that what you call fantasy is far more factual and truthful than most of you imagine."

"Please tell me more," I said, my interest piquing.

"It is not by chance that the worlds in those novels seem real to you. Now to burst the bubble of what constitutes fantasy. To call fantasy, fiction is a fallacy. People have it all wrong. Let me explain. You are first and foremost co-creators with me. If you can dream it and imagine it, then it is real for you. You have heard this saying often and use it frequently in your own counseling practice. I am here to tell you that many realities straddle, intermingle, and intertwine with each other, and there are countless numbers of them, although you are unconscious of them.

"There will always be a need for fantasy on yours and every world; what you call fantasy is very real on other planes and dimensions. Often times you are tapping your subconscious mind and accessing memories of lives that you lived so long ago in other eras and time periods that the memories have been relegated to the domains of myth, legend and fantasy. This makes them no less real or valid. Fantasy is so real that some of your finest writers are paid handsomely by the film industry (one of the greatest advocates and promoters of fantasy) to bring their creations and worlds to this world via audio sound and visual imagery – the picture on the screen. Words alone do not suffice to transport most people to other worlds. Until such time as humanity catches up with those brilliant ingenious souls who can experience many realities on the mental planes and hold the images and words and experience them in their minds, there will be the need for the physical props of visual imagery and audio resonances. The film industry – as long as it is convinced of the commercial value of such endeavors – is more than willing to supply the masses with stunning arrays of visual images and resonances so loud and piercing that blast your ears and brain from visual and audio overload.

"You may think that to embrace such ideas would shatter and rock your world and invite everyone into mindless escapism

through watching TV and viewing movies, or for the more
intellectually inclined, the reading of the books on which the
movies are based. Life on the Earth would be more enhanced and
take on more meaning if people were enlightened to the truth of
the mind and soul's participation with and creation of many
realities which exist, not separately, but simultaneously, right
alongside your everyday third dimensional reality.

"Your insane asylums would be virtually empty. You may
say that to encourage people to lose themselves in their mental
creations could lead to total moral chaos, social anarchy,
violence, and destruction. To lose oneself in a mental creation
and other worlds is not what I am advocating. To actively
participate, spend time and learn from the worlds of fantasy, I do
advocate.

"I personally would like to see more fantasy creations of
beautiful Eden like utopias than worlds where war, greed, and
injustice prevail. If you must create your dramas of good versus
evil and strong versus weak, intelligence versus weak
mindedness, at least learn to give equal footing to the 'goodness'
and the 'glories' of those who vanquish evil. Do not just
terminate your dramas with the 'They lived happily ever after'
type of endings. Show how they live happily ever after. Make
happiness come to life and give it breath through renewed
creation and expression with the wondrous mind that I have
bestowed upon each of you.

"Can I ever learn to give physical expression to my mental
fantasy creations that my mind fabricates? you may ask. The
answer is yes, but it is going to be quite some time before you
give 'physical life' to your fantasy creations such as you did in
olden times in ancient civilizations, many pre-Atlantean and pre-
Lemurian. But yes, you can, and this shall happen again. For
now, let's speak about how you manifest the things, situations,
and circumstances you wish to create around you. We have
spoken of this before, but repetition is a useful learning tool as I
have pointed out many times.

"All creation begins in the mind; such is the first rule of
creation. The masters and the adepts know this, and they always

create and hold mental images in their minds of what they intend to manifest on the physical realm. They understand a far greater physics, and possess knowledge of the laws of creation most people are not yet ready to know about, lest such knowledge and power be abused as it was in former civilizations.

"I have good news. The day is coming when you will have evolved to the point of being ready and trustworthy to once more possess the keys to 'creation'. Then your many worlds and creations will interact with one another, but not infringe upon each other. Until you make contact with the master souls who inhabit the higher dimensions, and your own higher self, you will be doomed to spend countless hours in front of the TV or computer in mental escapism.

"You will continue to live those 'quiet lives of desperation' which make me sad every time I see any of you with that blank look of boredom and apathy upon your face. Like me, you are able to experience and participate on many worlds, realms, and realities at the same time – although time is in reality an illusion. Before you can experience them, you must first perceive them. Your perceptions are your primary tools for your creations along with your beliefs, followed by your desires, goals and wishes and most important, your feelings.

"More people are beginning to believe that 'thoughts are things' and that what you can visualize you can manifest. It thrills me to see so many of you utilizing your thoughts to create what you intend and wish for, be it financial prosperity and abundance, good health, a happy relationship – what have you. Countless books have been written upon the magic potent forces that are released when you learn to harness the power of positive thinking.

"I say that this is grand and wonderful and I commend you for it. But some older souls are finding that such acquired skills and abilities are still not filling a void in their soul. They need more to make them complete and whole, or put another way, their soul needs to stretch and expand beyond the perimeters of third-dimensional confinement.

"Put more poetically, the soul needs and yearns to soar to other realms and worlds, which I might add, it frequently does during dream-time and night slumbers. Yet, being wed, for the time being, with the ego and the personality, it desires for the ego to ride and soar on its wings to visit and explore these worlds. Then upon returning, the memories may nourish both 'ego' and 'soul'.

"When soul and ego merge more fully and soar to heights beyond the Earth, then the gnawing claws of despair, loneliness, and apathy will not be able to reach them. Each day will be filled with joyous anticipation, and wonder-filled celebration of life will become constant. You are created and destined to be mavericks and pioneers of worlds great and small which exist inside and outside the perimeters of your physical being. If you are truly a part of All That Is (as All That Is – is a part of you), then you can visit the world of Luke Sky Walker that George Lucas created or the world of Captain Kirk that Gene Roddenberry created, just as easily as you can visit the worlds you explore in the fantasy and science fiction novels you read and explore in the realms of your own dreams.

"Be not so hasty to dismiss the imaginary fabrications of a ten year old boy playing alone or with friends in his back yard. Children are more apt than adults to take pleasure in stretching their creative imaginary muscles – that is to form images in their minds from the wellsprings of their own creative sub-conscious depths.

"Likewise, are your mental institutions full of creative persons who have lost themselves in the mental labyrinths of their own creations and explorations. Some are more content to remain there, secluded from society and the so-called 'real world'. You label them as 'crazy', but what is crazy, is your denial of the highly potent mental forces which enable them to wander beyond the limits of what the status-quo defines as 'acceptable reality'. Most of you believe that only what society collectively agrees upon and defines as reality is true, valid, and worthwhile. Such assessments are usually based upon exterior stimuli perceivable by the five physical senses. You see physical mass, matter, and objects with your eyes, hear sounds with your ears, and become smugly content that nothing beyond their perimeters can exist.

"I assure you, there are indeed countless realities existing at the present time, which exist for your exploration and enjoyment when you but heighten your perceptions. How do you do this? By awakening your mental and soul-faculties with the most marvelous tool I have endowed you with – your potent imagination. I earlier stated that many realities and worlds intermingle with one another. There are countless characters and plays within the panorama of your life experience, and I say this is a good thing. Your characters from other realms and worlds are as intrigued and interested in you and your particular world in which your ego inhabits, as you are in theirs. You are created to enhance one another's experiences and to improve each other's lives.

"As you help them evolve and grow, likewise, they do the same for you. How do you do this? You may ask. First, and most importantly, you acknowledge them and give them voice whenever they appear to you – be it in a dream or reverie, or just as an image that appears in your mind which you may be accustomed to dismissing as a figment of your imagination. A figment it may be – but a real one – and the more you acknowledge the images that appear in your mind, the more mental substance they take on, and the more real they become to you.

"There are countless exercises to utilize to awaken the imagination. Can you think of any?"

"Could one be to have someone take you on an imaginary journey to a special sacred place? They might create a suitable ambiance by turning the lights down and playing some soft, dreamy, ethereal music. They might present you with a hypnotic-induction, suggesting that you are totally relaxed and receptive to your soul and your imagination. They may offer suggestions for what a magical sanctuary might look like. It might take the form of a cave, an area by the ocean, or a setting in the forest."

"With practice, you will discover that your own imagination

will soon awaken and begin to supply you with additional images to help create your ideal setting – your special sanctuary you can visit anytime you choose. In time, to your delight, you will be introduced to a myriad of inner characters, play-mates, fantasy characters and friends, guides, mentors and guardian angels that are part of your soul family on the inner planes. Speaking of soul family, your guides have many gifts and treasures for you – the least of which is an amazing ability to magnify your hopes and dreams and to give you the needed mental energy and life-force to call them into physical manifestation. You can all surely recall times when you felt so clutched by despair and hopelessness that to get out of bed in the morning was a chore. Although you may have given into your despair at times and just stayed in bed all day, there were other times when you seemed to become aware of a different energy – even a presence – within you, and you noticed that this energy filled you with a glimmer of hope.

"This glimmer of hope was all it took to give you the strength to crawl out of the bed and to face yourself and the world yet another day. Call such a glimmer – that produced positive thoughts in your mind – your own mental, internal reservoirs of strength. Call it your own 'soul,' whispering to you. Call it someone from your inner soul family. Call it a friendly fairy, gnome, mermaid, guardian angel, spirit guide or even a departed loved one. It is all of this and much more.

"What is important, is that you call for help when in need, and to be receptive and willing to receive assistance in the countless infinite ways in which it can appear. Most people are not consciously aware of it, but many of the 'friendly voices' – who speak in your head and offer you encouragement – are beings who dwell within the landscapes and country sides of your inner realms and worlds. If you desire to become acquainted with your 'inner friends,' call upon them frequently, not just when in need. They enjoy your company. Many people call their friendly voices their spirit guide or 'guardian angels'. Many of your inner characters can and do play such roles.

"They have access to information that is usually very limited to most of you. An open mind, heart, and an active imagination all help you make contact with these guides. Too many people numb the soul with constant barrages of noise and distractions that keep the doors to your inner self closed. It is fine to enjoy movies, TV and books and the company of your friends. But do not forget your 'inner friends' – one of the greatest being your imagination. Dulled, numbed minds and bodies dim the soul's light and bar entry to the wonderful worlds within. This leads to boredom, restlessness, unhappiness and depression which leads to over indulging in vices. Make time for the silence and watch your creative muscles stretch and expand.

"You need not succumb to schizophrenic behaviors to become acquainted with your multi-dimensional self, although this happens to some unfortunate souls who charter the seas of their greater being prematurely, too hurriedly, or without proper guidance.

"Once you have learned to still your restless mind, you begin to hear the whispers of your intuition guiding you in positive directions. Is it really so difficult to slow your fast busy life-pace down to make time for meditation, reverie and musings? How can you hear the voice of your heart and soul if you are constantly plowing ahead at full speed, your mind, erratic thoughts and body moving hurriedly faster in a whirlwind of mindless distractions?

"Michael, I hope you now understand why I say that fantasy possesses elements of truth. You have not been able to completely bond with your writing because you have been confused as to how to draw the lines between truth and fiction, realism and fantasy. And I have not made things any easier by showing up one day and challenging and rocking your world, have I?"

"I suppose not, but you have shown up in person even if only in dreams. You have a tangible form. These morning visits over coffee are real."

Mr. Divine smiled. "Yes, we are back to that 'only a dream statement'. On a certain level, life on the Earth is 'only a dream' and yet it is so very real. Just like your fantasy characters and stories. Fact and fiction are opposite sides of the same coin; part of the duality of third-dimensional life. I will admit that your spirit guides and fantasy characters are not physically tangible. However, on other dimensions they are just as real as any person. They possess their own unique personalities, tastes, moods, ideas and interests.

"They are very connected to humanity and are very capable of stepping into your awareness via the wondrous portal you call the imagination. They can also make contact in dreams, reveries, meditations and other ways. Be honest with yourself, Michael, haven't you always felt in the deepest corners of your heart that your inner characters have a life of their own that goes beyond mere words in a notebook or on the computer?"

"Yes," I said, cautiously, "but I hardly believe that the psychiatrists would agree with me. They would probably say something to the effect that because I had an unhappy childhood, I became a loner and withdrew into my inner imaginary world of fantasy."

"That is excellent, and I totally agree with them. The reasons and how you get to 'the inner worlds' is irrelevant. What is important is that you went there. People go for different reasons. The only place I disagree is where they say that your inner imaginary worlds are not real...they are *very* real, have always been, and always will be. They just exist on different dimensions, and scientists tend to deny anything they cannot see, touch, feel, and label. That does not make your inner worlds less real; it merely means that others lack the perceptions and abilities to so far perceive the inner worlds. You and other creative people have developed the spiritual and imaginative soul faculties which enable you to make deeper contact. It is as simple as that.

"You possess the mark of an old soul, Michael ? you and some of your friends. This means that you have mental and spiritual access to realities, information, and knowledge unavailable to your everyday John Doe, so to speak. Being more curious and open-minded by nature, there is so much more that you can perceive, tune into and learn about. All of your fantasy and science fiction writers are old souls, but people like you are older still. Your typical fantasy writer can pour out stories and is content to label them as creations of their imaginations ? meaning they are make-believe or not real.

"You have tried to tell yourself that your 'writings' come from your muse – otherwise known as the voice of your inspiration. Most fantasy writers cannot believe their characters could be 'real,' other than characters from their imagination. You and a few others, on the other hand, sense and know in your soul, that there is more to characters than being simple 'imaginary figures'. I tell you, you are never going to be able to lose yourself in your writing of fantasy or science fiction until you come to terms with some plausible definitions that work for you. Michael, your mind is going to learn to accept my proposed new definitions and then, and only then, are you going to be able to get fired up once more and tell those fantasy stories that are germinating inside your head and imagination."

"Well, I suppose my readers are either going to take this step out on the limb with me, or they are going to run away and hope I get the help I need in some asylum because I have truly gone mad."

"It really does not matter what they think; what is important is that you receive the understanding you need so you can get back to your writing. Your writing is your therapy. You have never gone on anti-depressant medicines because you know that pills are not the answer. You have always believed that 'unexpressed, blocked repressed creativity' is the cause of your depression, and that is the truth."

"If for no other reason, my belief in fantasy has kept me off drugs. I guess there are more harmful things I could do."

"To deny or neglect the mind, imagination and the soul takes a tremendous toll on the person. There is good news, however. Since we are speaking about the imagination and the subconscious, let me add that far more people than you might realize do believe in the deeper implications of fantasy; otherwise, why would they keep the writers and the film industry in business?"

"Maybe they are just bored and need some escapism."

"That is part, but by no means, all of it, Michael. You know by now that you can be at odds with yourself about many things.

Everyone can. Discrepancies and duality exist in everyone to some degree. People may say they believe fantasy is only fiction, but some part of them, call it their inner child if you wish, believes otherwise. Walt Disney knew this and that is why his dream of Disney World came into manifestation for him. Talk about a master mind at work. People may say they don't believe in something, while part of them believes it, albeit this part subconscious. This can help you when you are struggling with your own beliefs about fantasy. You certainly have enough experience with your own self and the discrepancies of your own psyche to merit having some compassion and tolerance for others."

"I will never forget an experience that was pivotal in awakening my imagination. One day back in 1990, I was meditating with a friend who at one point placed his hands above my head and held them there for some time. I remember feeling this warmth radiating from his hands. I began feeling dizzy and tingles and strange sensations began pouring through me. I thought, at first, I might be dying. Everything began to feel so light and bright. I wanted to leave this world for good. I wanted to leave my body not knowing if such were even possible. It became more difficult to breathe. He must have sensed my discomfort because he removed his hands. I was speechless. He smiled and said that he gave me some energy. We talked for awhile then he left.

"He sure did a number on me. I lay still for about an hour trying to understand and assimilate what had occurred. To this day, I don't really know. I just know that he was somehow infusing energy into me and adjusting my mental or imaginary frequencies, whatever that means. Then I fell asleep for about two hours. When I woke up, I saw a woman dressed in bright white with stars in her eyes. There was a crown of stars on her head set next to dazzling rubies, diamonds and emeralds. I truly thought I was going crazy. The thought came to me to take out pen and paper. I did and my mind was flooded with torrents of strange phrases and words. Such was my personal induction into the realm of science fiction and fantasy and I wrote the beginning of my first science fiction story which, to this day, I never went back and finished although I have the scribbled notes somewhere."

"Actually this was not your first attempt at science fiction or fantasy writing. You wrote a story in your freshman year English class that had strong elements of science fiction in it, and you dabbled in horror and fantasy in a few others when you were much younger."

"I had forgotten about that. My main character in the science fiction story was called 'Dr. Time' and he was doing experiments in time travel. Wow. I guess I've been whacked longer than I thought," I said, grinning.

Mr. Divine let out a laugh. "In a sense, I guess you were. But it goes even further back. You were talking to fantasy characters when you were a child."

"Yes, I have vague memories of some of those times, but I just figured I made them all up."

"You did, and they were no less real since, I repeat yet again, that everything and everyone in your life experience is there because you created that experience and wanted them there at that particular time. You drew them to you just as people draw you into their life experiences. When there is mutual desire and need, then people enter into each other's worlds, real, fantasy-real, and otherwise."

"I'm afraid to get into 'otherwise' right now. I might really go off the deep end."

Mr. Divine chuckled. "We need not go there today. Let me just say that your friend was a conduit for you. He himself being very charged on the higher mental frequencies, was able to transmit some of that charge and transfer some of those energies into you. On a soul level, you were ready for such a breakthrough or you would not have drawn him into your life."

"I can accept that."

"Just as you draw like-minded people to you when the time is right, so do you attract like-minded inner characters when the time is right. Everyone has their purpose for coming into your life, as you do theirs. Never forget this and you are halfway up the road to enlightenment. To wind down this visit ? I wouldn't want you to blow any mental circuits as I know this conversation is one our most difficult ones so far. I now open the floor to you to share some of your experiences with some of your fantasy and inner characters. That is how we will end this visit."

"Okay. Let me see. I think the first fantasy character that comes to mind is Rosara, from the story I named after her. I will never forget her. I was writing a letter to my friend Janet one day, and at one point, I kinda zoned out and started writing about some lady from another planet and her soul mate. It's been so long since I read *Rosara*. What I do remember is that this boy spends a lot of time outside under a particular big tree. It is there that Rosara appears to him and takes him on a visit to her world. I recall one scene where the couple is holding hands and breathing in rose scented air, and I remember that instead of speaking, the people on that world communicate by singing.

"I was flabbergasted when I looked up and realized I had gone on that tangent in my letter to my friend Janet. A friend suggested that I submit the story to a publisher so I rewrote it and sent it to a few spiritual and New Age Magazines. None of them accepted the story, so I figured why not try some fantasy magazines. One accepted it and that was my first published story. *Rosara* has always haunted me. I remember talking to her many times even after I wrote the story; interesting enough, she would appear to me and talk back. The experience kind of scared me so I just stopped talking to her and dismissed her as a figment of my imagination."

"She was definitely more than that, and on some level you sensed it. So was that story about a higher, purer love?"

"You could say that."

"Were you dealing with love at that time of your life?"

"Most definitely. Some time before that I had written a piece, *The Messenger of Love*. It was similar to the theme of Rosara, but not as far out I'd say."

"Your soul brought Rosara to you. Do you know that? She comes from a realm where everyone's energy and love contributes to the collective rose-scented air that the couple breathed in."

"Yes, I do remember something like that taking place; they were drawing on the energy of the collective; their love was both personal and universal. That was something that really grabbed me about the story. I wanted to go to Rosara's world."

"Rosara's world does exist on another planet in another time and space continuum. You can go there anytime you wish via soul travel."

"I wish I had known that then."

"You would not have been so receptive then."

"I guess not, but nonetheless, that story, and how it just popped in so unexpectedly, blew me away. I wasn't even thinking about fantasy, love or anything related. I was just writing a letter to a friend and Rosara popped in. Now, that happens quite frequently. I guess I'm a conduit for beings all across the galaxy and universes. Or like I jokingly say, 'Schizophrenia beats dining alone.'"

"Everyone is schizoid to some degree and like I said, your soul brought Rosara to you. A deeper part of you knew of your struggle with love – as your soul knows of each and every struggle and heartache. It is your soul who brought you the angelic visitation at age thirteen and who made dream contact with the angel who taught you about unconditional love in the writing *The Messenger of Love*. Let's move on to another experience."

"After *Rosara,* I wrote a bunch of stories and began sending them out. No magazines bought any, but I got lots of exposure in small press magazines. During that time, other fairies, dragons, mermaids, you name it, creatures, beings, angels began appearing to me. One day when feeling real down, I lay on the couch and closed my eyes. A very handsome warrior with long golden hair appeared to me and invited me for a ride on his Pegasus for a ride to visit 'the sun people'. I know that sounds like some kind of drug-induced experience, but I was taking no drugs or even drinking. He looked just as real to me as my neighbor who would stop by for a visit sometimes. I forced myself to get out and do more things and meet new people, but my 'inner friends' still kept coming. Some would return frequently, others only came once."

"You were lucky to have such inner creative imaginative resources at your disposal."

"I believe that now, but had I been told so then, I would not have agreed. My rational side, my left brain, as I call it, threw some real big 'tizzies,' telling me that I was losing my mind and totally going off my rocker. So I would fight with my mind, telling it that as long as my 'inner friends' were not encouraging me to commit suicide or go out and murder anybody, there was nothing wrong with my visits. I insisted that there was probably a lot 'right' about them. My loneliness decreased drastically and I did a lot of writing. At one point, I had over one hundred pages of notes of ideas for different stories to write. Sometimes I'd spend every spare moment writing.

"It was then that I got the idea to aim higher ? to attempt a full-length novel. I started a couple, but couldn't get inspired enough to take them very far. Finally, Rolana appeared to me one day, saying, 'She was a young witch who indeed had a lot of women to save, and a lot to say." She was blunt and demanding. I liked her immediately and that novel kept me busy for several months. To my delight, a major publisher asked to read the manuscript. Although he did not buy my novel, that was at least a step in a new direction. I became exposed to the possibility of earning money and having a larger public reading my stories. That was something to look forward to, and when my mind would start in on me again, I'd say, 'Okay, so I'm writing fantasy, but if it can bring in an audience and some bucks, you got no right to complain.' Here I am ten years later talking to a whole variety of inner friends with no novel published."

"Hopefully, that is going to change for you, and one purpose of this visit is to help steer you in that very direction."

"It seems strange to think of fantasy having elements of truth, but when I think of truth being able to exist on many different levels, perhaps it makes more sense to me. What is real? is a question I have been asking most of my life so you have definitely stretched my mind and given me much to think about. I know there will be times I will think about this talk and think it is totally crazy, just like others who read it will think the same thing. Yet, there is always that part of me that says, 'Just what if he is right? Then what?'

"I wonder if my question of what is real began when I was a kid, trying to mentally escape 'the horrible goings on' at home. I'd often tell myself it was not real and do my best to pretend that it was not; maybe that was a survival mechanism for me. However, as time passed, I found myself asking the same thing when in disagreeable situations at school and other places. One day, I remember listening to the preacher at our church giving a sermon. I looked at him and I thought, is any of this real? Does anything he says really make one bit of difference? I'd struggle to memorize my multiplication tables and find myself asking, why am I learning this? Does it really matter? Does anything really matter?

"I recall that my restlessness would cease when I'd receive visits from my imaginary friends. Although I thought it was all made up, I still enjoyed those excursions. You'd think that I'd settle down and find my rightful place in the 'so-called real world,' but I never could. There was always that gnawing emptiness in me that would never go away. Although I got involved with my friends, with school activities and such, that lingering boredom was always close by. The funny thing is everybody thought I was normal. I excelled at most subjects and was constantly winning awards in school. I would act and sing in musicals and plays. I was on student council; I wrote for the student newspaper, defending this or that belief or the underdog. Everybody came to me for advice; the girls said they felt safe with me. I felt like a big brother to them and yet, the lingering boredom never completely went away.

"Sometimes, I'd just stare out into empty space with a blank look on my face. But being the chameleon that I was, I could snap out of it when I had to. If I was at church Bible school, at a picnic, or even playing ball, and lost myself in one of those empty stares, the children would yell, 'Come on, back to earth, Michael,' and I'd be right back and would go to bat, quote the Bible verse, or do whatever the situation called for.

"I think I have spent, and still spend much of my time longing and yearning for that which is beyond my scope. Some call it the yearning and search for the unattainable. I call it my 'there has to be more' moods, for that is truly what they are. I feel and sense in some part of my being that there is more – and much more – to life than I have seen. I used to play a game with myself when I was little called 'Looking for Mr. Invisible'. I'd pretend that he was out there somewhere, and I wanted to see him. I wanted to touch his shoulder to prove to myself that he had tangible form.

"In my game, he possessed magical powers and could perform phenomenal feats with his body and mind. He could take me to magical places and introduce me to all kinds of people, beings, and creatures that talked, danced, and sang. When I mentioned him to a teacher once, she just smiled and said I had been watching too much 'Alice in Wonderland'. From then on, I kept those experiences to myself and finally just blocked them out. But I could never block or chase away the lingering boredom and gnawing emptiness; they followed me everywhere. Maybe I am just destined to be eternally bored and never touch the unattainable because it is just that."

"And maybe not. Perhaps the unattainable has been trying to reach you all of your life. Maybe Mr. Invisible has been looking for you as well, but you have not looked hard enough to see him. It is not too late, Michael."

I yawned. "Well, this has been a wonderful visit, but I've had enough for now. My head is spinning so fast I feel like I am going to shred into a million pieces if we talk about this any longer. I need to come back to Earth and try to make some sense out of all of this."

Mr. Divine stood up and tipped his Boston Red Socks hat. "Life is a game, Michael. Try to never forget that. Don't take it too seriously or too lightly and you will come out a winner. Talk to you soon, sport," he said, and then disappeared into thin air. I saw an image of my childhood friend, Timmy Etherton. We were in the back yard playing. "It's your bat," he yelled, "why do you keep looking away? Come on and play the game, Mikey."

"Play the game," I uttered in my sleep.

Chapter Twenty-Four

A Visit to Mr. Divine's House

A few days passed before our next visit. I was immediately filled with a sense of joyous anticipation and knew that this visit would somehow be very special and different. Perhaps this was due to a radical change in Mr. Divine's attire. This time he wore a plain light brown robe with a white rope belt tied around his waist and instead of shoes, he wore beige sandals.

He lit up like a thousand light bulbs. We were both silent as I poured our morning coffee. The only sounds were our slurping and sipping. A time later, he reached out and took both my hands in his. His hands were so warm and strong. I felt like a little boy. I knew there would always be a little kid inside me that yearned for and needed a father. Mr. Divine grinned at me, then nodded his head as though in agreement. Sometimes, I wondered if I made up the visits for that very purpose. I thought of the movie *Jack Frost* where Michael Keaton plays the snowman dad. I had seen a poster about the movie that said: "A snow dad is better than no dad." That got a snicker from me. *Maybe a dream dad was better than no dad*, I thought. No matter what had been going on, I knew my mind would be pondering the visits for a long time. I also knew the visits were coming to an end. That made me sad. My divine guest looked at me long and deeply. His eyes glowed and I even thought I saw little stars in them.

A few minutes later, he moved a little closer to me and spoke softly. "Michael, I stick to my position when I say that fantasy is truth on other levels." Maybe I should have added that what is real and truthful on one level of reality may not seem real or truthful on another, but that does not make it any less real. Your inner characters and 'friendly voices' are very real on many different planes, and when you become more proficient at the art of soul travel, you are going to be able to move your consciousness, your mind, and your soul at will to many different planes, realms and worlds. You already do this to some degree, but you are still an apprentice, so to speak.

"For those who soul travel, you learn that time, space, the past, present and future are not encased in concrete boundaries. You will learn that you can be attracted to lots of people, places, and things and not know why, or not consciously know why, such as you were when you had your powerful deja-vu experiences in France. You were soul traveling to the past and tapping unconscious memories of not one, but several lives you lived there. Although it was not conscious, the memories were so powerful they jarred your subconscious to the point that the memories surfaced and spilled over into your conscious mind giving you intense deja-vu feelings.

"Your soul and spirit body know no limitations. Your spirit body is a light body, Michael; it is pure scintillating, brilliant light such as the paintings portray Jesus when he made his ascension. Your soul knows that viewing the stars, bright lights and your colorful Christmas lights serve as a reminder such as we have talked about before. So many people wander through lives like zombies, wondering who they are, and why they are here. They yearn for a light that never illuminates their darkness."

"I know," I said softly, "that is why I have dedicated my life to shedding what light I can onto others and helping all I can."

"How very honorable. That is also what I have been trying to do in these dream visits. Michael, I know you are struggling with these visits. We are going to call them to a halt for awhile so you can ponder them and sort things out. Your heart and your mind are going to be wrestling for awhile. You want to know if I am real to you and how real. I can tell you a million times that I am real, but your mind will still question and doubt. Such is part of the nature of the mind, one of its jobs, if you will. The issue here is what constitutes 'real' to you. I say that I am as real to you as your capacity to receive me is, and your capacity is much greater than you can ever begin to imagine. People need not be so hasty about naming what is delusion, fantasy, and imagination, and what is not. The inner and outer worlds are intertwined and enmeshed. There is nothing that you are not a part of. The inner world is meant to enhance, enliven, and empower the outer one. To step beyond the threshold of the third dimension is a gift when one does not do so solely as a means to escape the responsibilities of their everyday life. It is very possible to wander down the alleys and avenues of the outer and inner worlds. Exploring the inner realms is to make the journeys to the unconscious where untold knowledge and information dwell waiting to enrich and empower everyone.

"As your perceptions and soul faculties heighten, you begin to realize that 'inner' and 'outer' are but words, names and symbols of far greater realities. Your morning coffee has been delicious and I have enjoyed sampling every flavor that you have so kindly and graciously offered me. My company and the thoughts we have shared are very real, and it is my hope that you never forget them. More importantly, my love for you and for everyone is simply infinite, knowing no boundaries or limitations.

"If you think you are mad for claiming to have morning coffee with me in dreams, I say what is wrong with a little madness. You are all a little mad or have a few screws loose as the saying goes; otherwise, you could not even inhabit a physical body and partake of the human experience. Take comfort in your memories of our visits. I love you always."

Mr. Divine stepped up and threw his arms around me, giving me the biggest bear hug I had ever experienced. "When you are caught up being the adult and trying to figure everything out, just look in the mirror once in awhile and call out to that little boy inside you. He holds the keys to unlock all the treasures and magic inside and outside you. Cherish him and love him as I do. Hold him when he is sad. Laugh and play with him. Wander and explore worlds both inner and outer and give thanks for the beautifully complex, yet simple experiences of life."

He then kissed me on both cheeks. "We will visit France sometime together and check out their brews. In the meantime, keep the percolator in good running condition. You just never know when I will pop in again." Then he disappeared.

I woke up a little while later feeling restless and tired. Were our visits complete? "No," I said out loud, "This can't be the last one. Something is yet to be done. There is somewhere I must go.

"Home," I said softly. "Where is Mr. Divine's home? He has been visiting me here in my home in dreamtime for weeks. But where does he come from? Where does he go? How does he see the whole world and all that is in it from his window? Does he have windows? Can he imagine the spectacular view, the entire Earth, the entire world? Does he awaken to a choir of angels singing, and are there angels flying about? Is there sunlight? Is there darkness? Does he have a bed, and does he even sleep? Is there a floor, are there walls? Is there a view of 'Hell' and does it really exist? I want to see his paradise alive, dwell in the mainstream of his home. I'd love to take a walk with him, a walk to his home. How would I get there? How would I get back?"

My inquisitive mind wandered for what seemed hours. The questions, the endless phrases, were never ending in my mind. The next morning in the dream, Mr. Divine was blowing bubbles which then turned into clouds. His beautiful face with those mysterious, blue, penetrating eyes, covered the entire sky. "Where are you?" I asked.

"Tomorrow I will show you," he whispered then vanished.

The next morning he showed up as promised. I took in the aroma of Italian Roast coffee brewing in the kitchen. I quickly dressed and headed downstairs. Sure enough, there Mr. Divine sat, sipping his coffee. I helped myself to a cup. I put both hands around the mug and enjoyed the warmth; it took the bite off the crispy morn. I took a big swig; the coffee felt so good going down my throat. He looked at me with very somber eyes and waited patiently. He knew that I had something on my mind and he was right. The moment passed awkwardly as I mentally rehearsed what I wanted to say. No matter how I phrased it to myself, it kept sounding redundant.

I stammered, then got quiet, cleared my throat, but still the words did not come out. Finally he took a patient sip of coffee, warming his hands around the cup, and pleaded with his eyes for conversation.

I began, "I really enjoy our visits and I was wondering if I could come to your house for a visit? I mean, is that possible? Do I have to end my life on Earth before that can happen?" I kept stammering until he finally raised his right hand slightly, halting me from any further conversing or questioning.

"You are not asking the impossible," he stated matter-of-factly. "But first, tell me what you expect my home to look like," he remarked and then sat somewhat amused at his anticipation of my description.

Talk about being put on the spot, I felt as if the sky had fallen upon my shoulders. What did I expect? How did I picture the place? What do I say now? It seemed the ball was in my court.

"Okay," I will describe what I imagine your house looks like. Do I have your word that no matter what, the visit will be made possible?"

He gave one deep nod and I knew instantly that was his way of saying yes.

I talked about mansions, streets of gold, and other depictions and descriptions I had read in *The Bible* and heard in church as a kid. An old gospel song came to mind, "Mansions will glisten on the hills of glory, yet Jesus will outshine them all."

He said that I could visit his home the next morning and then he took his leave. I was so shocked and delighted. How could I even breathe? I was totally filled with excitement and anticipation for the rest of the day. My entire body felt like a locomotive and it was running full speed. When I went to bed, the minutes ticked away so slowly I thought I'd never fall asleep and yet I knew I had to. A time later I dozed off because when I opened my eyes, sounds were drifting to my room from my kitchen and he was here!

I hurriedly dressed and joined him in the kitchen. I expected him to be white robed, but of course I was wrong. He was dressed in a matching navy blue jogging suit which led me to believe that there was going to be lots of walking.

He took my hand and we were no longer in the kitchen. We were no longer anywhere, then darkness, total darkness, frozen fear of the unknown took over the locomotive in my stomach. My eyes automatically closed, my breath was labored. Then, just as suddenly as it began, it ended. Calmness filled my entire being, my eyes opened, and there we stood on a cloud looking at steps. How can I describe those steps? They seemed to be made of a watery substance, and they were endless.

"These steps are made of tears," he said. Suddenly, we were at the top of the steps, looking down at their endlessness. What were we standing on? There seemed to be no background; however, my feet were firmly supported. We began walking; it was slightly breezy, and it just suddenly appeared ? a rambling ranch. Meadows, old rock fencing, horses in a corral, a brook running into somewhat of a lake that nestled below a mountain in the far backside. The barn was dug into the lower hillside, and the wood frame house sat lodged at the top of the west hillside overlooking a play land for deer and creatures of the land. Kangaroos jumped about; I even think I saw a herd of sheep. Was I stunned? Actually, no. He really gave no impression that he would live anything but a simple, peaceful life.

Echoes were surrounding the entire atmosphere, yet we kept walking, walking, walking; the path kept getting longer; the house kept appearing further and further into the distance. Where is the feeling of love? I found myself thinking.

Finally, we arrived at the door; however, there was no door knob, no handle, nothing. How do we open the door? I wondered. We went around the house, and there was a fire pit, all aglow and inviting. He found a coffee pot, scooped water from the brook, and put the coffee grounds in and set it on a pole dangling over the hot embers. Soon the aroma of coffee filled the air.

We sat on the ground around the pit, drinking from plain old mugs. A deer wandered up and took a drink from the lake and lazily moved on. I could see a flock of wild turkey coming toward us. Did we have conversation? I am not sure because I seemed to just drift into the embers and take flight on sounds. I understood the misery of war and destruction; I knew the simplicity of peace and love, the fire of the dragons of deceit, and the calm of those that believed in the power of faith. It somehow all became real, the last sip of coffee now gone, the teary steps appeared again, and soon they were behind me in my descent. He looked at me with those deep penetrating eyes. I wanted to lose myself in those eyes; I felt they could take me to heights and depths yet unexplored. How I yearned to go there and explore untold worlds. Eternity seemed to be within my grasp. The experience became so intense that I almost passed out.

He gently approached me and placed his hand on my forehead. "It is time for me to take my leave now, Michael."

Feeling a bit choked up, I managed not to cry. "Goodbye, Mr. Divine," I said softly.

He smiled. "Not goodbye. The French, Italians, Germans and other cultures say it much better," he said, then waving said, "au revoir, arrivedererci, auf wiedersehen." Then he was gone.

A smile formed on the curve of my lips. "Yes," I whispered, "until we meet again, or literally 'until we see each other again.'"

I woke up still feeling dizzy. I drank some water, then sat in front of my fireplace. I knew that Mr. Divine's home would never be spoken about again. I asked, I received; I will forever live with the haunting realization of the indescribable!

Conclusion

Several months have passed since those profound visits with Mr. Divine; however, each and every one remains etched in my memories – the gestures, warming his hands around the steaming hot coffee cup, dressing in the tailored to casual wear, and finally, becoming reverent in the loose fitting robe, and simple robe belt with sandals of the handmade B.C. appearance.

His words forever fill the cavity of my brain. My thoughts continually drift back to those conversations. I have come to realize that the sum of my life is like the brilliant diamond snowflake on a blistery cold winter day, falling gently on my warm dewy nose, melting into a speck of moisture that blends and dries into nothingness. Is this the end or the beginning of the journey? I wonder, as I fold my hands together and raise them to lowered eyes and thoughtful face, and touch the tip of my nose in search of what was, what is and what can be.

About the Author

Michael Dennis has both local and national Media Exposure. He has been featured on FOX and CBS TV. He was featured on the Jerry Springer Show in 1991, and has appeared on numerous Radio Shows. In April 2000 he completed a six month Psychic Radio Show for MOJO 94.9 F.M. in Cincinnati. He has also been featured on WAIF 88.3 a.m. and on WSAI 1530 a.m. where he makes guest radio appearances. He was interviewed in the 2000 Millennium Edition of The Cincinnati Enquirer, The Pittsburgh Tribune, March 2003 the Columbus Dispatch, April 2005 and the Dayton Daily News in May 2008 for his Mother Teresa Channeling. He has been working Psychic Festivals and Fairs since 1986 in the mid-west as well as in Toronto and Ottowa Canada. Michael is also a writer and his first book Halfway to Heaven was published in 2003. His book of love poetry Dawn's Kiss, will be coming out in the summer or Fall of 2009.

One of Michael's earliest PSYCHIC EXPERIENCES is when he was a subject of the renowned Mentalist, "The Amazing Kreskin" at an oudoor Hypnosis Demonstration in Chautauqua, NY in 1977. Kreskin told Michael that he was unusually sensitive and he encouraged him to develop his psychic abilities.

Over the next several years after college Michael trained extensively and apprenticed with various Metaphysical Teachers. **In 1985, Michael became a professional Psychic.** In 1995 he gave up a foreign language teaching career to pursue his writing dream, and Psychic work full time.

In 1992 Michael began to expand his psychic work by publicly channeling Ascended Masters, Angels, Native American Ancestors and Shamans (Voices Of Our Ancestors), Benevolent Extraterrestrials and well-known beloved celebrities. He has publicly channeled The Blessed Mother Mary, Kuan Yin, Mary Magdalene, Archangel Michael, Nostradamus, Ascended Masters St. Germain and Hilarion, St. Francis, Helen Keller, Montezuma II Aztec Emperor, Sun Bear, Native American Medicine Shamans (Voices Of Our Ancestors), Fun and Frolic with the Faeries and a Past Life Exploration channeling with Vilura of Venus. He channeled Mother Teresa in Dayton in May 2008. Michael has tapes of all his channelings and sells them for $5 plus postage. He has begun to transcribe the tapes for a book called Wisdom From Beyond.

Michael is based in Cincinnati, OH, but has a world-wide clientele for Telephone and Email Readings.

To reach Michael please call:

513-281-5696

email: paxomnis@aol.com or mike@mikethepsychic.com

website: www.mikethepsychic.com

Other Books Published
by
Ozark Mountain Publishing, Inc.

Conversations with Nostradamus, Volume I, II, III.................by Dolores Cannon
Jesus and the Essenes..by Dolores Cannon
They Walked with Jesus..by Dolores Cannon
Between Death and Life... by Dolores Cannon
A Soul Remembers Hiroshima...by Dolores Cannon
Keepers of the Garden...by Dolores Cannon
The Legend of Starcrash...by Dolores Cannon
The Custodians..by Dolores Cannon
The Convoluted Universe - Book One, Two, Three..............by Dolores Cannon
Five Lives Remembered ....by Dolores Cannon
I Have Lived Before...by Sture Lönnerstrand
The Forgotten Woman..by Arun & Sunanda Gandhi
Luck Doesn't Happen by Chance...................................by Claire Doyle Beland
Mankind - Child of the Stars............................by Max H. Flindt & Otto Binder
The Gnostic Papers..by John V. Panella
Past Life Memories As A Confederate Soldier........................by James H. Kent
Holiday in Heaven...by Aron Abrahamsen
Is Jehovah An E.T.?..by Dorothy Leon
The Ultimate Dictionary of Dream Language..........................by Briceida Ryan
The Essenes - Children of the Light...............by Stuart Wilson & Joanna Prentis
Power of the Magdalene.................................by Stuart Wilson & Joanna Prentis
Beyond Limitations ....by Stuart Wilson & Joanna Prentis
Rebirth of the Oracle..............................by Justine Alessi & M. E. McMillan
Reincarnation: The View from Eternity......by O.T. Bonnett, M.D. & Greg Satre
The Divinity Factor...by Donald L. Hicks
What I Learned After Medical School ....by O.T. Bonnett, M.D.
Why Healing Happens...by O.T. Bonnett, M.D.
A Journey Into Being..by Christine Ramos, RN
Discover The Universe Within You...by Mary Letorney
Worlds Beyond Death...by Rev. Grant H. Pealer
Let's Get Natural With Herbs...by Debra Rayburn
The Enchanted Garden..by Jodi Felice
My Teachers Wear Fur Coats........................by Susan Mack & Natalia Krawetz
Seeing True...by Ronald Chapman
Elder Gods of Antiquity..by M. Don Schorn
Legacy of the Elder Gods..by M. Don Schorn
Reincarnation...Stepping Stones of Life ....by M. Don Schorn

Continue for more books by Ozark Mountain Publishing, Inc.

For more information about any of the above titles, soon to be released titles, or other items in our catalog, write or visit our website:

OZARK
MOUNTAIN
PUBLISHING

PO Box 754
Huntsville, AR 72740
www.ozarkmt.com
1-800-935-0045/479-738-2348
Wholesale Inquiries Welcome